Descendants
of
John Witt
the
Virginia
Immigrant

Robert W. Witt

HERITAGE BOOKS
2006

HERITAGE BOOKS
AN IMPRINT OF HERITAGE BOOKS, INC.

Books, CDs, and more—Worldwide

For our listing of thousands of titles see our website
at
www.HeritageBooks.com

Published 2006 by
HERITAGE BOOKS, INC.
Publishing Division
65 East Main Street
Westminster, Maryland 21157-5026

International Standard Book Number: 978-0-7884-0882-8

Contents

*1. **John Witt.** Born Circa 1645. Died Circa 1715 in Charles City
County, Virginia. Buried ? .

John's father is not known, nor is the place of his birth. Quite
possibly, he was born in Herefordshire, England, but this has not been
documented. Exactly when he arrived in Virginia is also not known, but
probably in the late1660's. The earliest reference to John Whitt is a land
patent dated 20 Nov 1670. Then in 1677 John Whitt served as a member
of a jury in Charles City County, VA (Whitt 325-326). Also, a Charles
City County Court Order in February1687 concerning the building of a
road refers to John Whitt's property as one of the lines (Weisiger, *Court
Orders*, 1687-1695, 23).

Information about the marriage and children is from Whitt (328-
331); *Harbour-Witt Bulletin* 6.2; Bates, "The Orphans."

He married Ann Daux, daughter of Walter Daux & Mary ?, Circa
1673 in Charles City County, VA. Born ? . Died ? . Ann's father,
Walter, was the son of Richard Daux, a London merchant. Walter
immigrated to Virginia as early as 1637. Ann's mother, Mary, first
married Robert Plaine, then Walter after Plaine's death, and John
Flowers after Walter's death. She had a son by Plaine, but apparently
had no children by Flowers (Bates, "The Orphans").

They had the following children:

2	i.	John Witt Jr.
3	ii.	William Witt
4	iii.	Edward Witt
5	iv.	Richard Witt
6	v.	Littlebury Witt

2. John Witt Jr. Born Circa 1675. Died Circa 1751 in Goochland County, VA.

John and his brother, William, purchased land in Henrico County, Virginia. The information about John's wife and children comes from Williams and Ross (601); *Harbour-Witt Bulletin* 6.2. Both sources list Lavinia as the wife's name, but both express uncertainty about the name. In 1730 a man named Rogers leaves a bequest in his will to his daughter Ann, wife of John Whitt (Weisiger, *Charles City County Wills and Deeds*, 40); both the Gendex report and Whitt (328) list Ann Rogers as his wife.

He married Ann Rogers, daughter of John Rogers & Elizabeth ?. Born ? . Died ? . They had the following children:

7	i.	Silvanus (Silas) Witt
8	ii.	Sarah Witt
9	iii.	John Witt III
10	iv.	? Witt
11	v.	? Witt

3. William Witt. Born Circa 1680. Died Jun 1754 in Albemarle County, Virginia.

William and his older brother, John, left Charles City County and purchased land in Henrico County from Charles and Mary Hudson. The deed, dated 13 Sept. 1715, specifies "300 acres on a fork of Tuckahoe Creek" (Weisiger, *Henrico County Deeds, 1706-1737*, 46). According to Graham, William gave half of this land to his son John in Octber of 1731. On 25 March 1738 William purchased from William Matlock of St. James Parish 200 acres on the "north side of North Fork of James River, bounded by the river, Ballengers Creek with all houses, etc." On

10 Aug. 1741, he also gave this tract to John "for love and affection" (Weisiger, *Goochland County Wills and Deeds, 1736-42*, 17, 64).

Information about the children is from *Harbour-Witt Bulletin*; Bates, E-Mail.

He married Mary ?. Born ? . Died 1741 in Albemarle County, Virginia. Buried in Albemarle County, Virginia. They had the following children:

12	i.	John Witt
✳ 13	ii.	Benjamin Witt
14	iii.	Sarah Witt
15	iv.	Agnes Witt
16	v.	Middy Witt

4. Edward Witt. Born Circa 1685. Died After 1752.

Information about the wife and children is from Chamberlayne (114, 116); Whitt (329).

He married Mary Eliza ?. Born ? . Died ? . They had the following children:

17	i.	Anne Witt
18	ii.	John Witt
19	iii.	William Witt
20	iv.	Mary Witt

5. Richard Witt. Born Circa 1690. Died Circa 1764 in Bute County, NC.

After living in Henrico, Amelia, and Halifx Counties in Virginia, Richard moved to Bute County, NC (*Harbour-Witt Bulletin* 6.2; Whitt 330). Information about the children is from the same sources. The *Harbour-Witt Bulletin* lists Mary Kimbrow as the only wife. The Gendex report, however, lists Elizabeth Liptrot as Richard's first wife. In a will dated 15 Nov 1734, Edmond Liptrot leaves a bequest to a daughter Elizabeth Whit (Weisiger, *Wills of Henrico County, 1654-1737*, 48). Whitt (330) indicates that the children, except for Edmund, are Elizabeth's. Edmund is the son of Mary.

He first married Elizabeth Liptrot. Born ? . Died ? . They had the following children:

21 i. Rev Richard Witt Jr.
22 ii. Hezekiah Witt
23 iii. John Witt
24 ? iv. Robert Witt Kimbrough

He second married Mary Kimbrow. Born ? . Died ? . They had the following children:

25 i. Edmund Witt

6. Littlebury Witt. Born ? . Died ? .

7. Silvanus (Silas) Witt. Born ? . Died ? .

Silvanus never married (Gendex).

8. Sarah Witt. Born 1695. Died After 1769 in Halifax, VA.

Information about the children is from *Harbour-Witt Bulletin* 6.2. The birth year for Sarah is from Gendex.

She married Thomas Harbour. Born ? . Died ? . They had the following children:

26	i.	Laminia Harbour
27	ii.	Talmon Harbour
28	iii.	Abner Harbour
29	iv.	Elisha Harbour
30	v.	Elijah Harbour
31	vi.	Adonijah Harbour
32	vii.	Mary Harbour
33	viii.	Jane Harbour
34	ix.	Sarah Harbour

9. John Witt III. Born ? . Died ? .

Information about the children (except David and Charles) is from *Harbour-Witt Bulletin* 6.2; information about David and Charles is from Bates, E-Mail.

He married Elizabeth ?. Born ? . Died ? . John was granted by patent on 17 Sept. 1731 400 acres on the south side of the James River. On 28 April 1734 he sold half of the tract to John Peter Bilboe and the other half to Peter Depp. Elizabeth, who co-signed the deed, signed her name Elizabeth P. Witt (Weisiger, *Goochland County Wills and Deeds, 1728-1736*, 52). The "P" may be from her maiden name.

They had the following children:

35	i.	John Witt IV
36	ii.	Mary Witt
37	iii.	Hannah Witt
38	iv.	Judah Witt
39	v.	Jesse Witt
40	vi.	Joyce Witt
41	vii.	David Witt
42	viii.	Charles Witt

10. ? Witt. Born ? . Died ? .

She married David Barnet. Born ? . Died ? (*Harbour-Witt Bulletin* 6.2).

11. ? Witt. Born ? . Died ? .

She married John Farrar. Born ? . Died ? (*Harbour-Witt Bulletin* 6.2).

12. John Witt. Born 1710. Died 1781. Buried in Amherst County, Virginia.

He married Lucy ?. Born ? . Died ? . Williams and Ross state that John first married a woman named Elizabeth and later married Lucy Littlebury, but they do not indicate which woman bore which children (602). Graham, on the other hand, indicates that John was married only once to Elizabeth Lucy Littlebury. The *Harbour-Witt Bulletin* 6.2 and Whitt (329) indicate only one wife named Lucy, maiden name unknown.

They had the following children:

43	i.	Littlebury Witt
44	ii.	John Witt Jr.
45	iii.	Abner Witt
46	iv.	Charles Witt
47	v.	George Witt
48	vi.	Elisha Witt
49	vii.	William E. Witt
50	viii.	David Witt

51   ix.   Lucy Witt

13. Benjamin Witt. Born Circa 1712. Died 1774.

Information about the children is from *Harbour-Witt Bulletin* 6.2; the date of daughter Marianne's birth is from *The Douglas Register* (385), and the marriage date is from Gendex.

He married Marianne Chastain, daughter of Jean Chastain & Charlotte Judith Amonet, Circa 1731. Born ? . Died ? . They had the following children:

52   i.   Marianne Witt Jr.

53   ii.   Benjamin Witt Jr.

54   iii.   John Witt

55   iv.   Charles Witt

56   v.   Lewis Witt

14. Sarah Witt. Born ? . Died ? .

She married John Canadey. Born ? . Died ? (Graham).

15. Agnes Witt. Born 1731 in Albemarle County, VA. Died 1788.

Information about Agnes, including her marriage and children, is from Gendex.

She married John Key Jr., son of John Key & Martha Tandy, 27 Dec 1750. Born 1731. Died 1789.

They had the following children:

57   i.   Elizabeth Key

58   ii.   Barbary Key

59   iii.   Judith Key

60   iv.   Winney Key

61   v.   William Key

62   vi.   John Waller Key

63   vii.   George Key

64   viii.   Joseph Key

16. Middy Witt. Born ? . Died ? .

She married Peter Chastain. Born ? . Died ? (*Harbour-Witt*

Bulletin 6.2).

17. Anne Witt. Born 11 Dec 1730 in Henrico County, VA. Died ? .

18. John Witt, Born 10 Jul 1734 in Henrico County, VA. Died Circa 1789 in Halifax County, VA. *Edward's child*

 Information about the wife and children is from Whitt (330).

 He married Ann ?. Born ? . Died ? . They had the following children:

65	i.	John Witt Jr.
66	ii.	Pool Witt
67	iii.	Peter Witt
68	iv.	William Witt
69	v.	Martha Witt
70	vi.	Ursilla Witt
71	vii.	Amey Witt
72	viii.	Mary Witt
73	ix.	Elizabeth Witt

19. William Witt. Born 1742. Died ? .

20. Mary Witt. Born 1745. Died ? .

21. Richard Witt Jr. Born ? . Died ? .

 Information about the wife and children is from *Harbour-Witt Bulletin* 6.2.

 He married Susannah Skaggs. Born ? . Died ? . They had the following children:

74	i.	Hezekiah Witt
75	ii.	Rachel Witt
76	iii.	Archibald Witt
77	iv.	Abijah Witt
78	v.	Edmund Witt
79	vi.	Ruthy Witt
80	vii.	Elizabeth Witt
81	viii.	Richard Witt III

22. Hezekiah Witt. Born ? . Died Circa 1790 in North Carolina.

   Information about the children is from *Harbour-Witt Bulletin* 6.2.

   He married ?. They had the following children:

82	✓ i.	Joshua Witt
83	ii.	Thenia Witt
84	✓ iii.	Burgess Witt
85	✓ iv.	Aires Witt
86	v.	William Rutherford Witt
87	✓ vi.	Lewis Witt
88	✓ vii.	Jesse Witt
89	viii.	David Witt
90	✓ ix.	Charles Witt

23. John Witt. Born ? . Died ? .

24. Robert Witt. Born ? . Died ? .

25. Edmund Witt. Born ? . Died ? .

   Information about the wife and children is from *Harbour-Witt Bulletin* 6.2.

   He married Ann ?. Born ? . Died ? . They had the following children:

91	i.	Anthony Witt
92	ii.	Edmund Witt Jr.
93	iii.	James Witt
94	iv.	John Witt
95	v.	William Witt
96	vi.	Henry Witt
97	vii.	Sallie Witt
98	viii.	Eggy Witt
99	ix.	Nancy Witt
100	x.	Rebecca Witt

26. Laminia Harbour. Born ? . Died ? .

She married Charles Witt, son of John Witt III & Elizabeth ?. Born ? . Died After 1771.

Information about the wife and children is from Williams and Ross (603).

They had the following children:

101	i.	Sarah Witt
102	ii.	Lavinia Witt
103	iii.	Mary Witt
104	iv.	Elijah Witt
105	v.	Charity Witt
106	vi.	Nelly Witt
107	vii.	Lydia Witt
108	viii.	Rhoda Witt
109	ix.	Susannah Witt
110	x.	Caleb Witt
111	xi.	Joseph Witt

27. Talmon Harbour. Born 1725. Died 1820 in Patrick, VA. .

He married Mary Wright. Born ? . Died ? (Lombardo).

28. Abner Harbour. Born ? . Died ? .

29. Elisha Harbour. Born ? . Died ? .

30. Elijah Harbour. Born ? . Died ? .

31. Adonijah Harbour. Born ? . Died ? .

32. Mary Harbour. Born ? . Died ? .

She married Palatiah Shelton. Born ? . Died ? (Lombardo).

33. Jane Harbour. Born ? . Died ? .

34. Sarah Harbour. Born 1732. Died 1814.

She married David Witt, son of John Witt III & Elizabeth ?. Born 1725 in Charles City County, VA. Died 1808 in Henry County, VA.

Information about the marriage and children is from Bates, E-Mail; Lombardo.

They had the following children:

112	i.	Mildred Witt
113	ii.	John Witt
114	iii.	Hannah Witt
115	iv.	Sarah Witt

35. John Witt IV. Born ? . Died ? .

Information about the marriage and children is from *The Douglas Register* (122, 322).

He married Mary Bullington, Circa 1753. Born ? . Died ? . They had the following children:

116	i.	Ann Witt
117	ii.	John Witt V
118	iii.	Mary Witt
119	iv.	Jeanie Witt
120	v.	Jesse Witt

36. Mary Witt. Born ? . Died ? .

Information about the marriage and the child is from *The Douglas Register* (148, 165).

She married John Bullington, Circa 1756. Born ? . Died ? . They had the following children:

121	i.	John Bullington Jr.

37. Hannah Witt. Born ? . Died After 1805.

Information about the marriage is from *The Douglas Register* (148); information about the children is from Gendex.

She married Charles Huddlesey, 2 Jul 1756. Born ? . Died ? . They had the following children:

122	i.	James Jennius Huddlesey

123	ii.	Charles Huddlesey
124	iii.	Parthenia Huddlesey
125	iv.	Jesse Huddlesey
126	v.	Adonijah Huddlesey
127	vi.	Adler Huddlesey
128	vii.	Elizabeth Huddlesey

38. Judah Witt. Born ? . Died ? .

Information about the marriage is from *The Douglas Register* (95).

She married John Matlock, 22 Nov 1756. Born ? . Died ? .

39. Jesse Witt. Born ? . Died ? .

40. Joyce Witt. Born ? . Died ? .

41. David Witt. Born 1725 in Charles City County, VA. Died 1808 in Henry County, VA.

Information about the marriage and children is from Bates, E-Mail; Lombardo.

He married Sarah Harbour, daughter of Thomas Harbour & Sarah Witt. Born 1732. Died 1814. They had the following children:

112	i.	Mildred Witt
113	ii.	John Witt
114	iii.	Hannah Witt
115	iv.	Sarah Witt

42. Charles Witt. Born ? . Died After 1771.

Information about the wife and children is from Williams and Ross (603).

He married Laminia Harbour, daughter of Thomas Harbour & Sarah Witt. Born ? . Died ? . They had the following children:

101	i.	Sarah Witt
102	ii.	Lavinia Witt
103	iii.	Mary Witt
104	iv.	Elijah Witt

105	v.	Charity Witt
106	vi.	Nelly Witt
107	vii.	Lydia Witt
108	viii.	Rhoda Witt
109	ix.	Susannah Witt
110	x.	Caleb Witt
111	xi.	Joseph Witt

43. Littlebury Witt. Born 1746. Died 1796.

Littlebury fought in the Revolutionary War (Lenora Sweeny 48). Information about the marriage is from William Sweeny (83).

He married Jenny Burnett, 30 Sep 1777 in Amherst County, VA. Born ? . Died ? .

The information about the daughters is based on my speculation from marriage records. A Milley Witt was married in December 1796 with the consent of her mother, Jean Witt. David Witt was Surety. Littlebury died in 1796 and hence the mother would need to give consent. David was a brother to Littlebury. A Polly Witt was married in 1800 with consent of her mother, Jinney Witt. The two girls apparently married brothers John and Charles Tooley or Tuley (Wm. Sweeny 77). Also, an Elizabeth Witt married in 1798 with the consent of her mother, Jean Witt (Wm. Sweeny 30). I have no other confirmation, though, that these are the daughters of Littlebury and Jenny Witt.

They had the following children:

129	i.	Millie Witt
130	ii.	Polly Witt
131	iii.	Elizabeth Witt

44. John Witt Jr. Born Circa 1753. Died 25 Aug 1825 in Knox County, TN.

John fought in the Revolutionary War and moved to Knox County, TN after the war. The information about the children is from Williams and Ross (602).

He married Elizabeth Luttrell, Circa 1770. Born ? . Died ? . They had the following children:

132   i.   Elizabeth Witt

133   ii.   Jesse Witt

134   iii.   John Witt III

135   iv.   Mary Witt

136   v.   Sarah Witt

137   vi.   Margaret Witt

138   vii.   Charles Witt

139   viii.   William Witt

140   ix.   Abner Witt

45. Abner Witt. Born Circa 1754. Died ? .

Abner fought in the Revolutionary War and moved to Knox County, TN, after the war (Williams and Ross 602). Abner was the heir at law to his brother Charles, a Continental soldier who died in the war (Lenora Sweeny 49).

He married Anna Churchill. Born ? . Died ? . They had the following children:

141   i.   Charles Wylie Witt

46. Charles Witt. Born Circa 1756. Died ? .

Charles was killed in the Revolutionary War (Bates, E-Mail).

47. George Witt. Born Circa 1758. Died ? .

George fought in the Revolutionary War and moved to Knox County, TN, after the war (Bates, E-Mail). In a petition in Amherst County, 17 May 1777, George requests reimbursement for expenses caused by sickness; he was a soldier in State and Continental service in June and July 1776 when he became ill (Lenora Sweeny 49). He married Betty ? (Williams and Ross 602).

48. Elisha Witt. Born 13 Sep 1759 in Albemarle County, VA. Died 16 Dec 1835 in Estill County, KY.

Elisha was drafted at age 17 to serve in the Revolutionary War.

He was present at the Seige of Yorktown and the surrender of Cornwallis. After the war he moved to Estill County, KY. All of his children were born and reared there (Graham).

He married Phoebe Dodd, 17 Jul 1781 in Estill County, KY. Born ? . Died 25 Apr 1855 in Estill County, KY. They had the following children:

142	i.	William Witt
143	ii.	Ann Witt
144	iii.	Charles Witt
145	iv.	Abner Witt
146	v.	Elisha Witt Jr.
147	vi.	Nathan Witt
148	vii.	Rachel Witt
149	viii.	David Witt
150	ix.	John Witt
151	x.	Silas Witt

49. William E. Witt. Born 20 Dec 1762 in Powatan County, VA. Died 26 Dec 1827 in Howard County, Missouri.

William fought in the Revolutionary War (Lenora Sweeny 48) and moved to Estill County, KY, after the war (Bates, E-Mail). Information about the wife and children is from Lombardo.

He married Mildred Baber, daughter of Thomas Baber & Elizabeth ?, 26 Dec 1782 in Albemarle County, VA. Born ? . Died ? . They had the following children:

152	i.	Elizabeth "Betsy" Witt
153	ii.	John Witt
154	iii.	Lucy Witt
155	iv.	Littlebury Witt
156	v.	Elisha Berry Witt
157	vi.	William E. Witt Jr
158	vii.	Obediah Witt

159	viii.	Mildred Witt Jr
160	ix.	Margaret Witt
161	x.	Nelson Witt
162	xi.	Mary "Polly" Witt

50. David Witt. Born ? . Died 28 Sep 1818 in Nelson County, VA.
Information about the wife and children is from Norton.
He married Sarah Abney. Born ? . Died ? . They had the following children:

163	i.	Dennet Witt
164	ii.	Ann Sparks Witt
165	iii.	David Witt Jr.
166	iv.	William Witt
167	v.	Cecilia Witt
168	vi.	Linnie Witt
169	vii.	Dice (Candice) Witt
170	viii.	Burgess Witt
171	ix.	Sally Witt

51. Lucy Witt. Born ? . Died ? .
She married Benjamin Carpenter. Born ? . Died ? (Williams and Ross 602).

52. Marianne Witt Jr. Born 19 Mar 1732. Died ? . *Beris Sen*

53. Benjamin Witt Jr. Born ? . Died ? .

54. John Witt. Born ? . Died ? .

55. Charles Witt. Born ? . Died ? .

✳ **56. Lewis Witt.** Born Circa 1730 in Ablemarle County, VA. Died 1774 in Bedford County, VA.
Information is from Gendex.
He married Anne Mills, daughter of William Mills & Mary ?, 1750. Born ? . Died ? . They had the following children:

| 172 | i. | John Witt |

57. Elizabeth Key. Born ? . Died ? .

58. Barbary Key. Born ? . Died ? .

59. Judith Key. Born ? . Died ? .

60. Winney Key. Born ? . Died ? .

61. William Key. Born Circa 1751. Died ? .

62. John Waller Key. Born 11 May 1752. Died 2 Dec 1827.
   He married Virginia Wade, 1775. Born ? . Died ? (Gendex).

63. George Key. Born 1753. Died ? .
   George's birth date is from Gendex.

64. Joseph Key. Born 1764. Died ? .
   Joseph's birth date is from Gendex.

65. John Witt Jr. Born ? . Died ? .
   Whitt (330) speculates that this William was the son of John, grandson of Edward, but this is not confirmed.
   He married ?. They had the following children:
   173   i.   William Witt

66. Pool Witt. Born ? . Died ? .

67. Peter Witt. Born ? . Died ? .

68. William Witt. Born ? . Died ? .

69. Martha Witt. Born ? . Died ? .

70. Ursilla Witt. Born ? . Died ? .

71. Amey Witt. Born ? . Died ? .

72. Mary Witt. Born ? . Died ? .

73. Elizabeth Witt. Born ? . Died ? .

74. Hezekiah Witt. Born ? . Died ? .
   He married Rachel ?. Born ? . Died ? (*Harbour-Witt Bulletin* 6.2).

75. Rachel Witt. Born ? . Died ? .
   She married ? Henderson. Born ? . Died ? (*Harbour-Witt Bulletin* 6.2).

76. Archibald Witt. Born ? . Died ? .
   He married Hannah Low. Born ? . Died ? (*Harbour-Witt*

77. Abijah Witt. Born ? . Died ? .

He married Elizabeth Elswick. Born ? . Died ? (*Harbour-Witt Bulletin* 6.2.)

78. Edmund Witt. Born ? . Died ? .

He married Hannah Lester. Born ? . Died ? (*Harbour-Witt Bulletin* 6.2).

79. Ruthy Witt. Born ? . Died ? .

She married Jesse Witt, son of Hezekiah Witt & ?, 10 Aug 1789. Born ? Died ? (*Harbour-Witt Bulletin* 6.2; Whitt 331).

80. Elizabeth Witt. Born ? . Died ? .

She married ? Cassidy. Born ? . Died ? (*Harbour-Witt Bulletin* 6.2).

81. Richard Witt III. Born ? . Died ? .

82. Joshua Witt. Born ? . Died ? .

He married Susan Sevier. Born ? . Died ? (*Harbour-Witt Bulletin* 6.2).

83. Thenia Witt. Born ? . Died ? .

She married Charles Sevier. Born ? . Died ? (*Harbour-Witt Bulletin* 6.2).

84. Burgess Witt. Born Circa 1760. Died ? .

Burgess fought in The Revolutionary War (*Harbour-Witt Bulletin* 6.2). Information about the wife from the same source.

He married Elizabeth Mayo. Born ? . Died ? .

85. Aires Witt. Born 1761. Died ? .

Aires also fought in The Revolutionary War (*Harbour-Witt Bulletin* 6.2)

86. William Rutherford Witt. Born ? . Died ? .

He married Hannah Munsey. Born ? . Died ? (*Harbour-Witt Bulletin* 6.2).

87. Lewis Witt. Born ? . Died ? .

88. Jesse Witt. Born ? . Died ? .

He married Ruthy Witt, daughter of Richard Witt Jr. & Susannah Skaggs, 10 Aug 1789. Born ? . Died ? (*Harbour-Witt Bulletin* 6.2; Whitt 331).

89. David Witt. Born ? . Died ? .

90. Charles Witt. Born 1776. Died ? .

91. Anthony Witt. Born Circa 1790 in Russell County, VA. Died 22 Jan 1862 in Lee County, VA.

Information about the wife is from *Harbour-Witt Bulletin* 6.2; information about the children is from Laningham (337-338); Lombardo.

He married Elizabeth Mace, 9 Aug 1806 in Surry County, NC. Born Circa 1790 in Russell County, VA. Died ? . They had the following children:

174	i.	Dora Witt
175	ii.	Edmond Witt
176	iii.	Sally Witt
177	iv.	Archibald Witt
178	v.	Martin Harrington Witt
179	vi.	Anthony Witt Jr
180	vii.	Robert Witt
181	viii.	Jonathan Witt
182	ix.	Elizabeth Witt

92. Edmund Witt Jr. Born ? . Died ? .

He married Sarah Cook. Born ? . Died ? (*Harbour-Witt Bulletin* 6.2).

93. James Witt. Born ? . Died ? .

94. John Witt. Born ? . Died ? .

He married Mary Pleasant. Born ? . Died ? (*Harbour-Witt Bulletin* 6.2).

95. William Witt. Born ? . Died ? .

He married Sally Sizemore. Born ? . Died ? (*Harbour-Witt*

Bulletin 6.2).

96. Henry Witt. Born ? . Died ? .

97. Sallie Witt. Born ? . Died ? .

She married William Moore. Born ? . Died ? *Harbour-Witt Bulletin* 6.2).

98. Eggy Witt. Born ? . Died ? .

She married Talton Branum. Born ? . Died ? (*Harbour-Witt Bulletin* 6.2).

99. Nancy Witt. Born ? . Died ? .

She married Lewis Franklin. Born ? . Died ? (*Harbour-Witt Bulletin* 6.2).

100. Rebecca Witt. Born ? . Died ? .

101. Sarah Witt. Born ? . Died ? .✓

    She married Henry Kirby. Born ? . Died ? (Williams and Ross 603).

102. Lavinia Witt. Born Circa 1745. Died Circa 1775 in Halifax County, VA.

    Information about the husband is from Williams and Ross (603); birth, death, and children from Gendex.

    She married Josiah Sullins, Circa 1767. Born ? . Died ? . They had the following children:

183	i.	Zachariah Sullins
184	ii.	Jesse Sullins
185	iii.	Joseph Sullins

103. Mary Witt. Born 4 Apr 1753. Died ? .

    Information about the husband is from Williams and Ross (603); birth date and son are from Gendex.

    She married Thomas Jarnigan Capt.. Born ? . Died ? . They had the following children:

186	i.	Jeremide Jarnigan

104. Elijah Witt. Born 1756. Died ? .

    Elijah fought in the revolutionary War (Lenora Sweeny 48). Elijah along with two brothers, Caleb and Joseph, and a sister, Mary (Polly ?), left Halifax County, VA, together and moved to Tennessee and settled about 1821 in Hamblen County, near Morristown (Williams and Ross 604). Information about the marriages and children from the same source. The Gendex report, however, indicates that Elijah died in 1801, and the *Harbour-Witt Bulletin* 6.2 indicates that Elijah married Jane Harbour.

He first married Nina Jarnigan Hutchinson. Born ? . Died ? .
They had the following children:

187 i.   Noah Witt
188 ii.   William Witt
189 iii. John Witt
190 iv.   Eli Witt
191 v.   Harmon Witt
192 vi.   Daniel Witt
193 vii. Polly (Mary ?) Witt
194 viii. Martha Witt

He second married Sally Bottom. Born ? . Died ? . They had the
following children:

195 i.   Piety Witt
196 ii.   Silas Witt
197 iii. Young ? Witt

105. Charity Witt. Born ? . Died ? .

She married Duncan Carmichael. Born ? . Died ? (Williams and
Ross 603).

106. Nelly Witt. Born ? . Died ? .

107. Lydia Witt. Born ? . Died ? .

Information about the husband and children is from Gendex.

She married William Maze. Born ? . Died ? . They had the
following children:

198 i.   Millie Maze

108. Rhoda Witt. Born ? . Died ? .

She married Thomas Stamps Sr.. Born ? . Died ? (Williams and
Ross 603).

109. Susannah Witt. Born ? . Died ? .

Information about the marriage is from Kathleen Williams (67). I
have no other confirmation that this Susannah Witt is the one David
Cosby married. According to the Gendex report, Susannah married

James Bates.

She married David Cosby, 24 Sep 1791 in Goochland County, VA. Born ? . Died ? .

110. Caleb Witt. Born 2 Sep 1762. Died 1827.

The information about the children is from Williams and Ross (603).

He married Miriam Horner, 2 Sep 1789. Born ? . Died ? . They had the following children:

199	i.	Elizabeth Witt
200	ii.	William Witt
201	iii.	James Witt
202	iv.	Charles Horner Witt
203	v.	Enoch Witt
204	vi.	Pleasant Witt
205	vii.	Samuel Witt
206	viii.	Merrill Witt
207	ix.	Coleman Witt

111. Joseph Witt. Born ? . Died 1824.

Information about the children is from Williams and Ross (603). Information about the wife and death date is from Gendex.

He married Sarah Kimbrough. Born ? . Died ? . They had the following children:

208	i.	Joseph Witt Jr.
209	ii.	Nathaniel Witt
210	iii.	Mourning Witt
211	iv.	Patsy Elizabeth Witt
212	v.	John Witt
213	vi.	James Witt
214	vii.	Res ? Witt
215	viii.	Silas Witt
216	ix.	Sally Witt

112. Mildred Witt. Born ? . Died Before 1820.

> She married Benjamin Moore, Circa 1770. Born ? . Died ? (Lombardo).

113. John Witt. Born Circa 1745. Died After 1826 in White County, TN.

> Information about John and his son is from Bates, E-Mail.

> He married Elizabeth ?. Born ? . Died ? . They had the following children:

> 217 i. Charles Witt

114. Hannah Witt. Born Circa 1755. Died ? .

115. Sarah Witt. Born Circa 1760. Died ? . *P. John III*

116. Ann Witt. Born 30 Aug 1753. Died ? . *P. John III*

> Information about the marriage is from Kathleen Williams (67). I have no other confirmation, though, that this is the Ann Witt Nowling married.

> She married Stephen Nowling, 6 Nov 1789 in Goochland County, VA. Born ? . Died ? .

117. John Witt V. Born 25 Dec 1756. Died ? .

118. Mary Witt. Born 18 Nov 1760. Died ? .

119. Jeanie Witt. Born 7 Mar 1763. Died ? .

120. Jesse Witt. Born 15 Jan 1766. Died ? .

121. John Bullington Jr. Born 4 Sep 1757. Died ? .

122. James Jennius Huddlesey. Born ? . Died ? .

123. Charles Huddlesey. Born ? . Died ? .

124. Parthenia Huddlesey. Born ? . Died ? .

125. Jesse Huddlesey. Born ? . Died ? .

126. Adonijah Huddlesey. Born ? . Died ? .

127. Adler Huddlesey. Born ? . Died ? .

128. Elizabeth Huddlesey. Born ? . Died ? .

129. Millie Witt. Born ? . Died ? .

> She married John Tooley, 10 Dec 1796 in Amherst County, VA.

Born ? . Died ? (William Sweeny 77).

130. Polly Witt. Born ? . Died ? .

She married Charles Tuley or Tooley, 6 Sep 1800 in Amherst County, VA. Born ? . Died ? (William Sweeny 77).

131. Elizabeth Witt. Born ? . Died ? .

She married Thomas Fitzpatrick, 22 Nov 1798 in Amherst County, VA. Born ? . Died ? (William Sweeny 30).

132. Elizabeth Witt. Born 5 Aug 1771. Died Feb 1863.

She married William Luttrell, 30 Jun 1787 in Amherst County, ✓ VA. Born ? . Died ? (William Sweeny 47).

133.√Jesse Witt. Born Circa 1776. Died 1846.√

Information about the marriage is from Kathleen Williams (108). I am not entirely certain that this is the Jesse Witt Betsy Martin married, but it would seem to be from the date and the fact that Benjamin Witt was the surety and J. Witt witnessed the marriage of another of Samuel Martin's daughters the next year. I also have added the children based on marriage records. J. Witt is listed as the father of Nancy, and she married James Hoge. Mary's father is listed as Jesse Witt, and Thomas Hoge was a witness. Mary married John Grinstead and John P. Witt married Catherine Grinstead (Hughes and Standefer 40,47, 111). I have no other confirmation, though, that they are the children of this Jesse Witt.

He married Betsy Martin, daughter of Samuel Martin, 10 Sep 1798 in Goochland County, VA. Born ? . Died ? . They had the following children:

  218 i. Nancy Witt

  219 ii. Mary Witt

  220 iii. John P. Witt

134. John Witt III. Born ? . Died ? .

135. Mary Witt. Born ? . Died ? .

136. Sarah Witt. Born ? . Died ? .

137. Margaret Witt. Born ? . Died ? .

138. Charles Witt. Born 1780. Died 1835.

139. William Witt. Born ? . Died ? .

William and Sally moved at some point to Madison County, KY (Norton). Information about the children is also from Norton.

He married Sally Witt, daughter of David Witt & Sarah Abney, 21 Nov 1810 in Nelson County, VA. Born ? . Died ? . They had the following children:

221	i.	Littleberry Witt
222	ii.	William Witt Jr.
223	iii.	? Witt
224	iv.	Jane Witt
225	v.	John Witt

140. Abner Witt. Born ? . Died ? .

141. Charles Wylie Witt. Born 1780 in North Carolina. Died 1835 in Hamilton County, TN.

Unless otherwise noted, all the information about Charles Wylie Witt and his descendants is from Larry Witt.

He married Amey Ellender (Alabama Alle) Gibson, 18 Mar 1800 in Knox County, TN. Born 1787 in Virginia. Died After 1860 in probably Putnam County, TN.

Alabama (Gibson) Witt was in the 1860 census of Putnam County, TN. She was living in the household with her daughter Ann Pendergrass (m. Jesse Pendergrass).

They had the following children:

226	i.	Jesse Witt
227	ii.	Gibson Witt
228	iii.	Ann Witt
229	iv.	Abner Lewis Witt
230	v.	James H. Witt
231	vi.	Almira Witt

232	vii.	Elnora Witt
233	viii.	John P. Witt
234	ix.	Rhoda G. Witt
235	x.	Samuel H. Witt Rev.
236	xi.	Mary (Polly) Witt
237	xii.	Charles Wylie Witt Jr.
238	xiii.	Allenson Witt

142. William Witt. Born 5 Sep 1782 in Estill County, KY. Died 30 Jan 1844.

Information about the marriage is from Lombardo; information about the children is from Graham.

He married Lucy Witt, daughter of William E. Witt & Mildred Baber, 20 May 1806 in Madison County, KY. Born 10 Feb 1788 in Albemarle County, VA. Died Jul 1859 in Estill County, KY.

They had the following children:

239	i.	Martha Witt
240	ii.	George Witt
241	iii.	Allen Witt
242	iv.	Louisa J. Witt
243	v.	Emalin Witt
244	vi.	James Witt
245	vii.	May Witt
246	viii.	Garland Witt
247	ix.	Lousinda Witt
248	x.	Delaney Witt
249	xi.	Malrinda Witt

143. Ann Witt. Born 29 Aug 1784 in Estill County, KY. Died ? .

144. Charles Witt. Born 21 Dec 1786 in Estill County, KY. Died 9 Mar 1871.

145. Abner Witt. Born 20 Feb 1789 in Estill County, KY. Died ? .

146. Elisha Witt Jr. Born 1 Feb 1792 in Estill County, KY. Died

1858.

147. Nathan Witt. Born 20 Oct 1794 in Estill County, KY. Died ? .

148. Rachel Witt. Born 19 Apr 1797 in Estill County, KY. Died ? .

149. David Witt. Born 27 Oct 1799 in Estill County, KY. Died ? .

150. John Witt. Born 27 Jan 1801 in Estill County, KY. Died 2 May 1826.

151. Silas Witt. Born 9 Sep 1803 in Estill County, KY. Died 31 Aug 1898.

Information about the marriage and children is from Graham.

He married Lucinda Darce Daniels, 28 May 1824. Born ? . Died 3 Mar 1888. They had the following children:

250	i.	James M. Witt
251	ii.	John M. Witt
252	iii.	Weeden M. Witt
253	iv.	Jincy Witt
254	v.	Wallace Witt

152. Elizabeth "Betsy" Witt. Born 25 Nov 1783 in Albemarle County, VA. Died 1852.

She married Joshua Mize, 1 Aug 1803 in Madison County, KY. Born ? . Died ? (Lombardo).

153. John Witt. Born 5 Nov 1785 in Albemarle County, VA. Died ? .

Information about the marriages is from Lombardo.

He first married Elizabeth Bybee, 24 Mar 1806 in Clark County, KY. Born ? . Died ? .

He second married Lucinda Meure, 10 Feb 1813 in Clark County, KY. Born ? . Died ? .

154. Lucy Witt. Born 10 Feb 1788 in Albemarle County, VA. Died Jul 1859 in Estill County, KY.

She married William Witt, son of Elisha Witt & Phoebe Dodd, 20 May 1806 in Madison County, KY. Born 5 Sep 1782 in Estill County, KY. Died 30 Jan 1844.

Information about the marriage is from Lombardo; information about the children is from Graham.

They had the following children:

239	i.	Martha Witt
240	ii.	George Witt
241	iii.	Allen Witt
242	iv.	Louisa J. Witt
243	v.	Emalin Witt
244	vi.	James Witt
245	vii.	May Witt
246	viii.	Garland Witt
247	ix.	Lousinda Witt
248	x.	Delaney Witt
249	xi.	Malrinda Witt

155. Littlebury Witt. Born 10 Dec 1789 in Albemarle County, VA. Died 15 Jan 1857 in Howard County, MO.

Information about the marriages and the son is from Lombardo.

He first married Fanny Hughs, 18 Jan 1814 in Estill County, KY. Born ? . Died ? . They had the following children:

255   i.   William Hughes Witt

He second married Susanna Tooley, 8 Jul 1823 in Boone County, MO. Born ? . Died ? .

156. Elisha Berry Witt. Born 24 Aug 1791 in Albemarle County, VA. Died 24 Feb 1829 in Howard County, MO.

He married Lydia George, 16 Aug 1816 in Clark County, KY. Born ? . Died ? (Lombardo).

157. William E. Witt Jr. Born 20 Jan 1794 in Albemarle County, VA. Died ? .

Information about the marriages is from Lombardo.

He first married Mary Parker, 15 Apr 1818 in Franklin, KY. Born ? . Died ? .

He second married Jane Cox, 27 Nov 1822 in Madison County, KY. Born ? . Died ? .

158. Obediah Witt. Born 1 May 1796 in Albemarle County, VA. Died ? .

159. Mildred Witt Jr. Born 14 Jun 1798 in Albemarle County, VA. Died ? .

She married William Carson, 22 Apr 1809 in Madison County, KY. Born ? . Died ? (Lombardo).

160. Margaret Witt. Born 19 Dec 1800 in Estill County, KY. Died 22 Jun 1885 in Jewell, KS.

She married John Martin Lile, 15 Aug 1819 in Howard County, MO. Born ? . Died ? (Lombardo).

161. Nelson Witt. Born 27 Dec 1802 in Estill County, KY. Died 13 Aug 1863.

He married Catherine McConkle, 22 Sep 1822 in Howard County, MO. Born ? . Died ? (Lombardo).

162. Mary "Polly" Witt. Born 15 Jan 1805 in Estill County, KY. Died 27 Oct 1880 in Fresno County, CA. Buried in Oak Knoll Cemetery, Oakhurst, CA.

Information about the marriage and children is from Lombardo.

She married William Fletcher Newton, son of Kenneth Newton & Martha Feemster, 29 Jun 1822 in Howard County, MO. Born ? . Died ? .

They had the following children:

256	i.	Mandy Newton
257	ii.	W. Harrison Newton
258	iii.	Martha Ann Newton
259	iv.	Elizabeth Katherine Newton
260	v.	Louisa Newton
261	vi.	F. Marion Newton
262	vii.	Caroline Newton

263	viii.	Margaretta Newton
264	ix.	Mary Catherine Newton
265	x.	Napoleon B. Newton

163. Dennet Witt. Born Circa 1771. Died 1840.

Information about the marriage is from William Sweeney (83). Information about the children is from Norton.

He married Constance Christian Oglesby, daughter of Richard Oglesby, 4 Jan 1790 in Amherst County, VA. Born ? . Died 1850. They had the following children:

266	i.	John Witt
267	ii.	Malinda Witt
268	iii.	Dicie Witt
269	iv.	Catherine (Kittie) Witt
270	v.	Sallie Witt
271	vi.	Ann S. Witt
272	vii.	Susan Witt
273	viii.	Nancy Witt
274	ix.	William Witt
275	x.	David Witt

164. Ann Sparks Witt. Born ? . Died ? .

She married Samuel Fitzpatrick, 18 Jun 1792 in Amherst County, VA. Born ? . Died ? (William Sweeney 29).

165. David Witt Jr. Born ? . Died 26 Jan 1866.

Information about the children is from Norton; Baldridge (13).

He married Jane Fitzpatrick, 10 Sep 1810 in Nelson County, VA. Born ? . Died ? . They had the following children:

276	i.	Sallie Witt
277	ii.	Mary Jane Witt
278	iii.	David Witt III
279	iv.	William Witt
280	v.	Susanna Witt

281   vi.   Eliza Witt

166. William Witt. Born ? . Died 1836.

Information about the children is from Norton; Bates, E-Mail.
Information about the marriage is from Vogt and Kethley (68).

He married Frances Fitzpatrick, 4 Dec 1810 in Nelson County,
VA. Born ? . Died ? . They had the following children:

282   i.   John E. Witt
283   ii.   David Witt
284   iii.   James Witt
285   iv.   Frances J. Witt

167. Cecilia Witt. Born ? . Died ? .

Information about the marriage is from William Sweeney (57).
Information about the children is from Norton.

She married Jesse Oglesby, 15 Sep 1794 in Amherst County,
VA. Born 15 Sep 1794. Died ? . They had the following children:

286   i.   Nancy Oglesby
287   ii.   Sarah Oglesby

168. Linnie Witt. Born ? . Died ? .

She married Daniel Wade, 4 Oct 1798 in Amherst County, VA.
Born ? . Died ? (Baldridge 5).

169. Dice (Candice) Witt. Born ? . Died ? .

Information about the children is from Norton; the wedding date
is from Baldridge (5).

She married William Hamlet, 17 Sep 1809 in Nelson County,
VA. Born ? . Died ? . They had the following children:

288   i.   Sally Hamlet
289   ii.   David Hamlet
290   iii.   Archelaus Hamlet

170. Burgess Witt. Born 1783. Died Mar 1873.

Information about the wife and children is from Norton.

He married Nancy Strickland. Born ? . Died ? . They had the following children:

 291 i. John W. Witt
 292 ii. Hezikiah Witt
 293 iii. Nancy Candice Witt
 294 iv. Abigail Witt
 295 v. Sarah Ann Witt

171. Sally Witt. Born ? . Died ? .

  She married William Witt, son of John Witt Jr. & Elizabeth Luttrell, 21 Nov 1810 in Nelson County, VA. Born ? . Died ? . They moved at some point to Madison County, KY (Norton). Information about the children is also from Norton. They had the following children:

 221 i. Littleberry Witt
 222 ii. William Witt Jr.
 223 iii. ? Witt
 224 iv. Jane Witt
 225 v. John Witt

172. John Witt. Born 1769 in Bedford County, VA. Died 1808.

  Information about the wife and son is from Gendex.

He married Kizzie Ann ?. Born ? . Died ? . They had the following children:

 296 i. Robert L. Witt

173. William Witt. Born 1756 in Halifax County, VA. Died ? .

  Information about the children is from Whitt (330).

He married ?. They had the following children:

 297 i. John Witt
 298 ii. Pool Witt
 299 iii. Seth Witt
 300 iv. Hezekiah Witt
 301 v. David Witt
 302 vi. William Witt Jr. 5.

303　vii.　Sarah Witt

304　viii.　Nancy Witt

305　ix.　Tabitha Witt

174. Dora Witt. Born ? . Died ? .

175. Edmond Witt. Born 1810 in Russell County, VA. Died 31 May 1870 in Lee County, VA.

Information about Edmond, including marriage and children is from Laningham (337-338) and Lombardo.

He married Annie Thompson, 22 Dec 1831 in Lee County, VA. Born 27 Nov 1812. Died 11 Aug 1882. They had the following children:

306	i.	Elizabeth Witt
307	ii.	Rebecca Witt
308	iii.	William Witt
309	iv.	John Witt
310	v.	Alfred Witt
311	vi.	Mary Ann Witt
312	vii.	Archibald Witt
313	viii.	Martha Witt
314	ix.	Margaret Witt
315	x.	Child Witt
316	xi.	Jasper Franklin Witt

176. Sally Witt. Born Circa 1814 in Russell County, VA. Died ? .

Information about the marriage and children is from Lombardo.

She married Ori G. Collier, 21 Apr 1834 in Lee County, VA. Born ? . Died ? . They had the following children:

317	i.	Nancy Collier
318	ii.	Didama Collier
319	iii.	John Collier
320	iv.	David Collier
321	v.	William Collier
322	vi.	Elizabeth Collier

323	vii.	McMullin Collier
324	viii.	Mahala Ann Collier

177. Archibald Witt. Born 1818 in Russell County, VA. Died ? .
Archibald went to Kentucky ca. 1837, stayed until ca. 1847, and
then returned to Russell County, VA (Laningham 337-338); information
about the wife and children is also from Laningham and Lombardo.

He married Rachel Kelly, daughter of Isaac Kelly & Cynthia
Parker, 31 Jan 1837 in Harlan County, KY. Born ? . Died ? . They had
the following children:

325	i.	Isaac Witt
326	ii.	Edmond Witt
327	iii.	Anna Witt
328	iv.	Cynthia Witt
329	v.	John Witt
330	vi.	Martha Witt
331	vii.	Emeline Witt
332	viii.	Mary Witt

178. Martin Harrington Witt. Born Feb 1820 in Russell County,
VA. Died 22 Feb 1906 in Lee County, VA.

Information about the wives and children is from Laningham
(337-338) and Lombardo.

He first married Louisa Osborne, Circa 1845. Born ? . Died ? .
They had the following children:

333	i.	Andrew Jackson Witt
334	ii.	Wiley M. Witt
335	iii.	Latticia Witt
336	iv.	Ambrose Witt
337	v.	James D. Witt
338	vi.	Eli Witt
339	vii.	Martha Witt
340	viii.	Robert Witt

341	ix.	Nancy Witt
342	x.	Mary Witt

He second married Martha Elizabeth Clarkson, Circa 1867. Born ?. Died ?. They had the following children:

343	i.	Sarah Francis Witt
344	ii.	Cynthia Witt
345	iii.	Ira G. Witt
346	iv.	Nellie C. Witt

179. Anthony Witt Jr. Born 1821. Died ?.

Information about the wife and children is from Laningham (337-338).

He married Luscinda Clarkston, daughter of Thomas Clarkston & Ellender Feathers. Born 1813 in Lee County, VA. Died ?. They had the following children:

347	i.	Jacob Witt
348	ii.	Prissa Witt
349	iii.	Archable Witt
350	iv.	Elizabeth Witt
351	v.	James Witt
352	vi.	Lavinia J. Witt
353	vii.	Andrew Witt
354	viii.	William Witt

180. Robert Witt. Born 1827. Died ?.

Information about the wife and child is from Lombardo.

He married Lucy ?. Born ?. Died ?. They had the following children:

355	i.	Edward Witt

181. Jonathan Witt. Born Apr 1830 in Lee County, VA. Died ?.

Information about the wives and children is from Laningham (337-338) and Lombardo.

He first married Susan Holmes, 1850 in Harlan County, KY.

Born ? . Died ? . They had the following children:

356	i.	Nancy Witt
357	ii.	Elizabeth Witt
358	iii.	Emeline Witt
359	iv.	Rebecca Witt
360	v.	Mary Ann Witt
361	vi.	John Witt

He second married Barbary Short, daughter of James Short & Rebecca Bailey, 1867 in Harlan County, KY. Born ? . Died ? . They had the following children:

362	i.	Charles Witt

182. Elizabeth Witt. Born Circa 1833 in Lee County, VA.

183. Zachariah Sullins. Born ? . Died ? .

184. Jesse Sullins. Born ? . Died ? .

185. Joseph Sullins. Born ? . Died ? .

186. Jeremide Jarnigan. Born ? . Died ? .

187. Noah Witt. Born 16 Mar 1776. Died ? .

He married Millie Maze, daughter of William Maze & Lydia Witt,
3 May 1794 in Jefferson County, TN. Born ? . Died ? (Gendex).

188. William Witt. Born Circa 1778. Died Circa 1780.

The date of death is from Gendex.

189. John Witt. Born 18 Apr 1780. Died ? .

He married Eleanor Penny. Born ? . Died ? (Williams and Ross
604).

190. Eli Witt. Born 10 Aug 1785. Died ? .

He married Nancy McNealy, 13 Jul 1806 in Jefferson County,
TN. Born ? . Died ? (Williams and Ross 604; Gendex).

191. Harmon Witt. Born 16 Oct 1789 in Jefferson County, TN. Died
21 Dec 1830 in Polka County, IL.

Information about the wife is from Williams and Ross (604); all
other information is from Gendex.

He married Miriam Skeen, 23 Dec 1807. Born ? . Died ? . They
had the following children:

363   i.   Anderson Witt

192. Daniel Witt. Born 22 Jun 1790. Died ? .

He married Injabo Skeen, daughter of John Skeen & Catherine
White, 3 Apr 1813 in Jefferson County, TN. Born ? . Died ? (Williams
and Ross 604; Gendex).

193. Polly (Mary ?) Witt. Born Circa 1792. Died ? .

William was the son of Sally Bottom, Elijah's second wife (Williams and Ross 604). The date of the marriage is from Gendex.

She married William Bottom, 15 Jul 1806 in Jefferson County, TN. Born ? . Died ? .

194. Martha Witt. Born ? . Died ? .

She married Martin Gentry. Born ? . Died ? (Williams and Ross 604).

195. Piety Witt. Born ? . Died ? .

Information about the husband is from Williams and Ross (604). The date of the marriage is from Gendex.

She married Silas Gentry, 18 Apr 1814 in Jefferson County, TN. Born ? . Died ? .

196. Silas Witt. Born Circa 1800. Died ? .

197. Young ? Witt. Born ? . Died ? .

198. Millie Maze. Born ? . Died ? .

She married Noah Witt, son of Elijah Witt & Nina Jarnigan Hutchinson, 3 May 1794 in Jefferson County, TN. Born 16 Mar 1776. Died ? (Gendex)

199. Elizabeth Witt. Born 14 Apr 1790. Died ? .

200. William Witt. Born 26 Jul 1795. Died ? .

201. James Witt. Born 14 Feb 1796. Died ? .

202. Charles Horner Witt. Born 5 Jun 1797. Died ? .

203. Enoch Witt. Born ? 5 Dec . Died ? .

204. Pleasant Witt. Born 18 Feb 1800. Died ? .

205. Samuel Witt. Born 6 Jun 1806. Died ? .

206. Merrill Witt. Born 17 Apr 1807. Died ? .

207. Coleman Witt. Born 26 Feb 1816. Died ? .

208. Joseph Witt Jr. Born ? . Died ? .

He married Sarah Earle. Born ? . Died ? (Williams and Ross 603).

209. Nathaniel Witt. Born ? . Died ? .

He married Mary Cate, 1804. Born ? . Died ? (Williams and Ross 603).

210. Mourning Witt. Born ? . Died ? .

211. Patsy Elizabeth Witt. Born ? . Died ? .

She married Charles Sevier. Born ? . Died ? (Williams and Ross 603).

212. John Witt. Born ? . Died ? .

213. James Witt. Born ? . Died ? .

214. Res ? Witt. Born ? . Died ? .

215. Silas Witt. Born ? . Died ? .

216. Sally Witt. Born ? . Died ? .

She married Edward Sellers. Born ? . Died ? (Williams and Ross 603).

217. Charles Witt. Born 18 Apr 1775. Died 26 Apr 1848 in Barren County, KY.

Information about the marriage and children is from Bates, E-Mail; Gorin, *Bible and Family Records* (315).

He married Nancy Logan, daughter of William Logan & Agnes McCown, 29 Oct 1801 in Lincoln County, KY. Born ? . Died ? . They had the following children:

364	i.	Jane Witt
365	ii.	Polly Witt
366	iii.	Elizabeth Witt
367	iv.	Nancy Witt
368	v.	Jarusha Witt
369	vi.	John Witt
370	vii.	William Logan Witt
371	viii.	Benjamin F. Witt
372	ix.	Unnamed Witt
373	x.	Julia Ann Witt

374	xi.	Unnamed Witt
375	xii.	Charles Foster Witt
376	xiii.	Andrew Jackson Witt
377	xiv.	Catherine H. Witt
378	xv.	Emily M. Witt

218. Nancy Witt. Born ? . Died ? .

She married James Hoge, 2 Aug 1820 in Goochland County, VA. Born ? . Died ? (Hughes and Standefer 47).

219. Mary Witt. Born ? . Died ? .

She married John E. Grinstead, 26 Jan 1829 in Goochland County, VA. Born ? . Died ? (Hughes and Standefer 40).

220. John P. Witt. Born ? . Died ? .

He married Catherine Grinstead, daughter of William Grinstead, 20 Aug 1828 in Goochland County, VA. Born ? . Died ? (Hughes and Standefer 111).

221. Littleberry Witt. Born 10 Feb 1811 in Culpeper County, VA. Died ? .

222. William Witt Jr. Born ? . Died ? .

223. ? Witt. Born ? . Died ? .

She married James Naylor. Born ? . Died ? (Norton).

224. Jane Witt. Born ? . Died ? .

She married William Rhodes. Born ? . Died ? (Norton).

225. John Witt. Born ? . Died ? .

John lived in Madison County, KY for a time, but moved to Illinois in 1853 (Norton; also source for marriage and children).

He married Amanda Berge, 1836. Born ? . Died ? . They had the following children:

379	i.	Amelia Witt
380	ii.	Sarah Witt
381	iii.	David William Witt
382	iv.	John R. Witt

383	v.	Lucy Ellen Witt
384	vi.	Eliza Witt
385	vii.	Fannie Witt
386	viii.	Alice Witt
387	ix.	Mary Witt

226. Jesse Witt. Born ? . Died ? .

227. Gibson Witt. Born 28 Jun 1801 in Knox County, TN. Died After 1860 in Knox County, TN.

He married Rebecca Mateson, Circa 1828. Born 1805. Died ? . They had the following children:

388	i.	Mateson M. Witt
389	ii.	Adoline Witt
390	iii.	Jerimah Witt
391	iv.	Mary Witt
392	v.	Elizabeth Witt
393	vi.	Ginna Witt
394	vii.	Allen Witt
395	viii.	John Witt
396	ix.	Ellen Witt

228. Ann Witt. Born Circa 1805 in Tennessee. Died ? .

She married Jesse Pendergrass, Circa 1825. Born Circa 1806 in South Carolina. Died ? . They had the following children:

397	i.	Jesse Pendergrass Jr.

229. Abner Lewis Witt. Born 15 Feb 1814 in Blount County, TN. Died ? .

Lived in Fentress County, TN, according to the 1850 Census. He married Elizabeth Yeager, 1850 in Fentress County, TN. Born 1818. Died ? . They had the following children:

398	i.	Charles L. Witt

230. James H. Witt. Born 1815 in Blount County, TN. Died ? .

Amey Ellender, age 63, was a part of James's household in

Hamilton County, TN, according to the 1850 Census.

He married Jane Bryant, Circa 1849 in Hamilton County, TN. Born 1817. Died ? . They had the following children:

- 399   i.   Sarah A. Witt
- 400   ii.   Mary A. Witt

231. Almira Witt. Born Circa 1816. Died ? .

She married ? Mayo. Born ? . Died ? .

232. Elnora Witt. Born Circa 1817 in Blount County, TN. Died ? .

Other possible names are Elmore, Elmira, Almiry Mayo. She married David Mayer. Born ? . Died ? .

233. John P. Witt. Born 1817 in Blount County, TN. Died ? .

He married Celia Moore, Circa 1837 in Hamilton County, TN. Born 1819. Died ? . They had the following children:

- 401   i.   James Witt
- 402   ii.   Alabama Witt
- 403   iii.   Charles Witt
- 404   iv.   Mary Witt
- 405   v.   Samuel Witt
- 406   vi.   Almyra Witt
- 407   vii.   John Witt

234. Rhoda G. Witt. Born 18 Nov 1818. Died 28 Mar 1888 in Hamilton County, TN.

She married George Varner. Born 5 Mar 1816. Died 4 Jun 1902. They had the following children:

- 408   i.   Nancy Ann Varner
- 409   ii.   James J. Varner
- 410   iii.   Mary Alabama Varner
- 411   iv.   Sarah Varner
- 412   v.   John Varner
- 413   vi.   Ester Varner
- 414   vii.   Sophronia Varner

415 viii. Elizabeth Varner

235. Samuel H. Witt Rev. Born 4 Dec 1820 in Blount County, TN.
Died 16 Feb 1885 in Taylor County, KY. Buried in Union Ridge
Cemetery.

He married Sarah Jane Varner, Circa 1842. Born 1824 in
Hamilton County, TN. Died 1896 in Taylor County, KY. Buried in
Union Ridge Cemetery. They had the following children:

416	i.	Mary A. Witt
417	ii.	Adolphus (Dof) Witt
418	iii.	Maria E. Witt
419	iv.	Elizabeth B. Witt
420	v.	James D. Witt
421	vi.	Chelf Witt
422	vii.	Melissa A. Witt
423	viii.	Charles Lewis Witt
424	ix.	Wesley Randolph Witt
425	x.	Vestina A. Witt
426	xi.	Victoria Witt
427	xii.	Emily (?) Witt

236. Mary (Polly) Witt. Born Circa 1821.

She married John Hodges. Born ? . Died ? .

237. Charles Wylie Witt Jr. Born 19 Jul 1823 in North Carolina.
Died ? in Fentriss County, TN.

He married Phoebe Emiline Yeager, 10 Nov 1847 in Putnam
County, TN. Born 1825 in North Carolina. Died ? in Fentriss County
TN. They had the following children:

428	i.	Eliza A Witt
429	ii.	Sarah J. Witt
430	iii.	John A. Witt
431	iv.	Mary E. Witt
432	v.	Martha C. Witt

433   vi.   Levina E. Witt

238. Allenson Witt. Born Circa 1826. Died ? .

He first married Sara J. Rogers. Born ? . Died ? .

He second married Ann Yeager, 10 Oct 1847. Born Circa 1827. Died Circa 1865.

239. Martha Witt. Born ? . Died ? .

She married Joe Durham, 20 Dec 1849. Born ? . Died ? (Graham).

240. George Witt. Born ? . Died ? .

Information about the wife and children is from Graham.

He married Louisa Webb. Born ? . Died ? . They had the following children:

434	i.	William Witt
435	ii.	Amanda Witt
436	iii.	James H. Witt
437	iv.	Rebecca Witt
438	v.	Dean Witt
439	vi.	John V. Witt
440	vii.	Polly Ann Witt
441	viii.	Jefferson Witt
442	ix.	Phoebe Ann Witt

241. Allen Witt. Born 12 Feb 1813 in Estill County, KY. Died Jun 1883 in Estill County, KY.

Information about the marriage is from Graham; information about the children is from Gendex. It would seem that either Graham is mistaken about the date of the marriage or that Gendex is mistaken about the dates of the births of the first three children. I, however, have simply recorded the dates as I found them.

He married Mary B. "Polly" Cox, 25 Jan 1845. Born ? . Died ? . They had the following children:

443   i.   Cynthia Witt

444	ii.	William Witt
445	iii.	Clayborn Witt
446	iv.	Thomas Jefferson Witt
447	v.	Isaiah Witt
448	vi.	David H. Witt
449	vii.	Nancy E. Witt
450	viii.	John Witt
451	ix.	James M. Witt
452	x.	Jesse Witt
453	xi.	Asa Witt
454	xii.	Elizabeth Witt

242. Louisa J. Witt. Born ? . Died ? .

She married Merida King, 8 Apr 1845. Born ? . Died ? (Graham).

243. Emalin Witt. Born ? . Died ? .

She married Richard Barns, 5 Feb 1835. Born ? . Died ? (Graham).

244. James Witt. Born 8 Feb 1818. Died 4 Apr 1897.

Information about the marriage and children is from Graham.

He married Lavinia Jane Dunaway, 23 Jul 1842. Born 6 Feb 1825. Died 1 Jan 1903. They had the following children:

455	i.	John W. Witt
456	ii.	George R. Witt
457	iii.	Sarah L. Witt
458	iv.	Benjamin J. Witt
459	v.	Hester Jane Witt
460	vi.	David Nelson Witt
461	vii.	Henry Clayton Witt

245. May Witt. Born ? . Died ? .

She married Stuart Barnett. Born ? . Died ? (Graham).

246. Garland Witt. Born ? . Died ? .

Information about the marriage and children is from Graham.

He married Louisa Griggs, 9 Jan 1838. Born ? . Died ? . They had the following children:

462	i.	Josepha Witt
463	ii.	Louvinia J. Witt
464	iii.	Milda Witt
465	iv.	Barthena Witt
466	v.	Sarah J. Witt
467	vi.	Francis Witt
468	vii.	Ellen Witt
469	viii.	Louisa Ann Witt
470	ix.	McClellan Witt

247. Lousinda Witt. Born ? . Died ? .

She married John Barns. Born ? . Died ? (Graham).

248. Delaney Witt. Born ? . Died ? .

Information about the wife and children is from Graham.

He married Nancy Johnson. Born ? . Died ? . They had the following children:

471	i.	Emaline Witt
472	ii.	William Witt
473	iii.	Fannie Witt
474	iv.	H. M. Witt
475	v.	Sarah Witt
476	vi.	Delaney Witt Jr.
477	vii.	Charley Witt
478	viii.	Clabe Witt

249. Malrinda Witt. Born ? . Died ? .

Malrinda never married (Graham).

250. James M. Witt. Born 6 Apr 1825. Died 1888.

251. John M. Witt. Born 25 Sep 1826. Died 13 Mar 1903.

Information about the wife and children is from Graham.

He married Emaline A. Jacobs, daughter of Nathan Jacobs & Burilla Whitney. Born 24 Nov 1839. Died 11 Jul 1912. They had the following children:

479	i.	Sarah Ella Witt
480	ii.	Issac N. Witt
481	iii.	William L. Witt
482	iv.	Lousinda Burilla Witt
483	v.	Eugene Witt

252. Weeden M. Witt. Born 16 Jun 1832. Died ? .

253. Jincy Witt. Born 21 Jun 1834. Died ? .

She married Ansil D. Powell, 29 Oct 1851. Born ? . Died ? (Graham).

254. Wallace Witt. Born 6 Jun 1837. Died ? .

255. William Hughes Witt. Born 1819 in Madison County, KY. Died ?

256. Mandy Newton. Born 4 Sep 1823 in Howard County, MO. Died ?

She married Caswell Overton, 20 Mar 1842. Born ? . Died ? (Lombardo).

257. W. Harrison Newton. Born 15 Oct 1825 in Howard County, MO. Died ? .

258. Martha Ann Newton. Born 7 May 1828 in Howard County, MO. Died ? .

259. Elizabeth Katherine Newton. Born 13 Apr 1830 in Randolph County, MO. Died Circa 1899 in Fresno County, CA.

Information about the marriages is from Lombardo.

She first married Henry H. Hickman, 30 Mar 1849 in Dallas County, TX. Born ? . Died ? .

She second married J. R. Nichols. Born ? . Died ? .

260. Louisa Newton. Born 2 Feb 1832 in Howard County, MO. Died ?

261. F. Marion Newton. Born 8 Nov 1833 in Howard County, MO. Died ? .

262. Caroline Newton. Born 25 Jan 1842 in Howard County, MO. Died ? .

263. Margaretta Newton. Born 21 Nov 1839 in Howard County, MO. Died ? .

264. Mary Catherine Newton. Born 25 Jan 1842 in Howard County, MO. Died ? .

265. Napoleon B. Newton. Born 9 Feb 1844 in Howard County, MO.

266. John Witt. Born ? . Died ? .

He married ? Roberts, in Nelson County, VA. Born ? . Died ? (Norton).

267. Malinda Witt. Born ? . Died ? .

She married John Nelson Burnett, Nov 1825 in Nelson County, VA. Born ? . Died ? (Vogt and Kethley 126).

268. Dicie Witt. Born ? . Died ? .

She married John W. Witt, son of Burgess Witt & Nancy Strickland, 28 Jan 1822 in Nelson County, VA. Born ? . Died 18 Jun 1872.

Information about the marriage is from Vogt and Kethley (126); information about the children is from Norton.

They had the following children:

484	i.	Asa William Witt
485	ii.	Jesse David Witt
486	iii.	Dennet Abner Witt
487	iv.	John Witt
488	v.	Sallie Witt
489	vi.	Connie Witt

490   vii.   Nanny Witt

269. Catherine (Kittie) Witt. Born ? . Died ? .

She married Ellis Strickland, 19 Mar 1834 in Nelson County, VA. Born ? . Died ? (Vogt and Kethley 126). According to Norton, Ellis and Catherine moved to West Virginia.

270. Sallie Witt. Born ? . Died ? .

271. Ann S. Witt. Born ? . Died ? .

She married David Rippetoe, 28 Apr 1834 in Nelson County, VA. Born ? . Died ? (Vogt and Kethley 126). According to Norton, David and Ann moved to Vigo County, IN.

272. Susan Witt. Born ? . Died ? .

Information about the marriage is from Vogt and Kethley (126); information about the children is from Norton.

She married Uriah Hatcher, 20 Mar 1821 in Nelson County, VA. Born ? . Died ? . They had the following children:

    491   i.   John Hatcher

    492   ii.   Lavinia Hatcher

    493   iii.   Hilery Hatcher

    494   iv.   Abner Hatcher

273. Nancy Witt. Born ? . Died ? .

She married John Noel, in Bedford County, VA. Born ? . Died ? (Norton).

274. William Witt. Born ? . Died ? .

He first married ? Oberchain. Born ? . Died ? (Norton).

He second married Polly Hatcher. Born ? . Died ? (Norton).

He third married Mary Jones. Born ? . Died ? (Norton).

He fourth married Mary Hass. Born ? . Died ? (Norton).

275. David Witt. Born ? . Died ? .

Information about the marriage and children is from Norton.

He married Martha A. Douglas, daughter of David Douglas, 31 Jan 1838 in Bedford County, VA. Born ? . Died ? . They had the following children:

495	i.	William E. Witt
496	ii.	David H. Witt
497	iii.	Robert R. Witt
498	iv.	Bettie D. Witt
499	v.	Laminia Witt
500	vi.	Charlie M. Witt

276. Sallie Witt. Born ? . Died ? .

She married Andrew McCreary, in Nelson County, VA. Born ? . Died ? (Vogt and Kethley 126).

277. Mary Jane Witt. Born ? . Died ? .

She married Augustus Rice, 14 Sep 1838 in Nelson County, VA. Born ? . Died ? (Vogt and Kethley 126).

278. David Witt III. Born 15 Jul 1811. Died ? .

David served in the War between the States (Baldridge; information about the marriage also from Baldridge).

He married Elizabeth Jones, 22 Mar 1847 in Nelson County, VA. Born ? . Died ? . They had the following children:

501	i.	George D. Witt
502	ii.	Charles Witt
503	iii.	Thomas Witt
504	iv.	John Witt
505	v.	Sallie Witt

279. William Witt. Born ? . Died ? .

William moved to Ohio (Norton). Information about the marriage is from Vogt and Kethley (68).

He married Virginia P. Jones, 25 May 1846 in Nelson County, VA. Born ? . Died ? .

280. Susanna Witt. Born ? . Died ? .

She married Alfred Pettit. Born ? . Died ? (Baldridge 13).

281. Eliza Witt. Born ? . Died ? .

She married Alfred C. Pettit, 8 Jan 1851 in Nelson County, VA. Born ? . Died ? (Baldridge 13).

282. John E. Witt. Born ? . Died ? .

He first married Susan T. Murphey, 20 Jan 1835 in Nelson County, VA. Born ? . Died ? (Vogt and Kethley 68).

He second married Adeline Newton. Born ? . Died ? (Norton).

283. David Witt. Born ? . Died ? .

According to Norton, David married Janet Wade. However, in the marriage records of Nelson County, compiled by Vogt and Kethley, The David Witt who married Janetta Wade on 19 Dec 1836 is David Witt, Jr. (67). It seems more likely that this David is the David Witt who married Candice E. Warwick on 18 Jan 1836 in Nelson County (Vogt and Kethley 67). According to Norton, David and his wife had no children.

He married Candice E. Warwick, 18 Jan 1836 in Nelson County, VA. Born ? . Died ? .

284. James Witt. Born 1 Jun 1818 in Nelson County, VA. Died 11 May 1888 in Allen County, KY. Buried in Maynard, New Bethel Church Cemetery.

James' first child was born in Virginia in 1837, but his second child (b. 1840) was born in Kentucky. James, thus, moved to Kentucky shortly before 1840; he is listed in the Allen County Census for 1840. After coming to Kentucky, James purchased land from his uncle William Fitzpatrick (Deed Book G, 483; H, 278;), K. D. Dorsey (Deed Book H, 523), Fletcher Gatewood (Deed Book G, 432), and John Wolfe (Deed Book H, 530). Later he purchased more land from Herman and Reaves Whitney (Deed Book M, 154). Before 1865 he owned at least 350 acres close to Lym Camp Creek and Rhoden Creek. He also apparently owned a store; his will directs that the contents of his store be sold.

Unless otherwise noted, the information about the Witts from Allen County, KY, comes from Allen County, KY, Cemeteries; Allen

County, KY, Census Records; Allen County, KY, Marriage Records; Allen County, KY, Tax Lists; and Kentucky Vital Statistics. Information about the first marriage is from Vogt and Kethley (67).

He first married Elizabeth Martin, 30 Nov 1835 in Nelson County, VA. Born Circa 1814. Died 1860/1865 in Allen County, KY. Elizabeth is listed with James in the 1860 Census, but in 1865 James married Nancy E. Braswell. Thus Elizabeth apparently died sometime after 1860 but before 1865.

They had the following children:

506	i.	Martha Elizabeth F. Witt
507	ii.	William H. Witt
508	iii.	Sidney W. Witt
509	iv.	John F. Witt
510	v.	Luther H. Witt

He second married Nancy E. Braswell, daughter of Ely C. Braswell & Sarah Stockton, 7 Aug 1865 in Allen County, KY. Born 19 Mar 1846 in probably in Clinton County, KY. Died ? (Watkins).

James and Nancy E. had no children.

285. Frances J. Witt. Born ? . Died ? .

She married James Fitzpatrick, 13 Jan 1838 in Nelson County, VA. Born ? . Died ? (Vogt and Kethley 126).

286. Nancy Oglesby. Born ? . Died ? .

287. Sarah Oglesby. Born ? . Died ? .

288. Sally Hamlet. Born ? . Died ? .

289. David Hamlet. Born ? . Died ? .

290. Archelaus Hamlet. Born ? . Died ? .

291. John W. Witt. Born ? . Died 18 Jun 1872.

Information about the first marriage is from Vogt and Kethley (126); information about the children and second wife is from Norton.

He first married Dicie Witt, daughter of Dennet Witt & Constance Christian Oglesby, 28 Jan 1822 in Nelson County, VA. Born ? . Died ? .

They had the following children:

484	i.	Asa William Witt
485	ii.	Jesse David Witt
486	iii.	Dennet Abner Witt
487	iv.	John Witt
488	v.	Sallie Witt
489	vi.	Connie Witt
490	vii.	Nanny Witt

He second married Elizabeth Hight. Born 9 Sep 1823. Died May 1921. They had the following children:

511	i.	Camden Hezikiah Witt
512	ii.	Daniel Kirk Witt
513	iii.	Florence Witt
514	iv.	Josephine Cornelia Witt
515	v.	Candice (Dicie) Witt

292. Hezikiah Witt. Born 5 Apr 1817. Died ? .

Hezikiah moved to Missouri in 1840 (Norton; also source for wife and children).

He married Jane Bates, 15 Feb 1838 in Charlottesville, VA. Born ? . Died ? . They had the following children:

516	i.	Roland Witt
517	ii.	Sarah Ann Witt
518	iii.	John M. Witt
519	iv.	Nancy Witt

293. Nancy Candice Witt. Born ? . Died ? .

She married James William Rittenhouse, 9 Apr 1839 in Nelson County, VA. Born ? . Died ? (Vogt and Kethley 126).

294. Abigail Witt. Born ? . Died ? .

Information about the marriage is from Vogt and Kethley (126); information about the children is from Norton.

She married Thomas Dickenson, 22 Jan 1844 in Nelson County,

VA. Born ? . Died ? . They had the following children:

    520   i.   Ella Dickenson

    521   ii.   Louise Dickenson

    522   iii.   Christie Dickenson

295. Sarah Ann Witt. Born ? . Died ? .

Information about the marriage is from Vogt and Kethley (126); information about the children is from Norton.

She married John C. Collins, 23 Oct 1837 in Nelson County, VA. Born ? . Died ? . They had the following children:

    523   i.   Elizabeth Collins

    524   ii.   Addison Collins

    525   iii.   Samuel Collins

    526   iv.   John Collins

296. Robert L. Witt. Born ? . Died ? .

Information is from Gendex.

He married Dorcas Willis, daughter of John Willis & Jane Kirkpatrick, 28 Feb 1825 in Hamilton County, IL. Born ? . Died ? . They had the following children:

    527   i.   Kizzie Ann Witt

    528   ii.   John Wesley Witt

    529   iii.   Sarah Jane Witt

    530   iv.   William Witt

    531   v.   Miles Witt

297. John Witt. Born ? . Died ? .

298. Pool Witt. Born ? . Died ? .

299. Seth Witt. Born ? . Died ? .

300. Hezekiah Witt. Born ? . Died ? .

301. David Witt. Born ? . Died ? .

302. William Witt Jr. Born 1787. Died ? .

303. Sarah Witt. Born ? . Died ? .

304. Nancy Witt. Born ? . Died ? .

305. Tabitha Witt. Born ? . Died ? .

306. Elizabeth Witt. Born 1832. Died 1911.

307. Rebecca Witt. Born Circa 1835. Died Circa 1865.

She married James Clarkston, 4 Dec 1856 in Lee County, VA. Born ? . Died ? (Laningham 337-338).

308. William Witt. Born 5 Jun 1837 in Lee County, VA. Died Feb 1922 in Wise County, VA.

Information about the wife and children is from Laningham, who indicates that William and Elizabeth had eleven children but lists only two of them (337-338); Lombardo adds four more.

He married Elizabeth Clarkston, daughter of James Clarkston & Mary Morris, 25 Jun 1857 in Lee County, VA. Born ? . Died ? . They had the following children:

532	i.	Martha Jane Witt
533	ii.	Alpha E. Witt
534	iii.	Docia Witt
535	iv.	Mary A. Witt
536	v.	James M. Witt
537	vi.	John B. Floyd Witt

309. John Witt. Born 1840. Died 1918.

He married Rachel Couch, 3 May 1867 in Lee County, VA. Born ? . Died ? (Lombardo).

310. Alfred Witt. Born 1843. Died ? .

Information about the marriage and child is from Lombardo.

He married Martha Morison, 20 Feb 1868 in Lee County, VA. Born ? . Died ? . They had the following children:

538	i.	John H. Witt

311. Mary Ann Witt. Born 1845. Died 1881.

She married Henry H. Clarkson. Born ? . Died ? (Laningham 337-338).

312. Archibald Witt. Born 1848. Died ? .

Archibald moved to Oklahoma (Laningham 337-338); information about the wife and child is from Lombardo.

He married Sarah Ann Spencer, daughter of Armstrong Spencer & Nancy Profitt. Born ? . Died ? . They had the following children:

539   i.   James Monroe Witt

313. Martha Witt. Born 1853. Died ? .

She married Marion Morris. Born ? . Died ? . (Laningham 337-338).

314. Margaret Witt. Born 1853. Died ? .

315. Child Witt. Born 1855. Died ? .

316. Jasper Franklin Witt. Born 25 Jan 1857 in Keokee, VA. Died 7 Mar 1936.

Information about the wife and children is from Laningham (337-338).

He married Dora Hurst, daughter of William Hurst & Eliza Sprinkle, 17 Aug 1885 in Tazewell, TN. Born ? . Died ? . They had the following children:

540   i.   Eliza Kate Witt
541   ii.   Carrie E. Witt
542   iii.   Roy M. Witt
543   iv.   Earnest Clyde Witt
544   v.   Hazen Hurst Witt
545   vi.   Infant Witt
546   vii.   Edgar Kennedy Witt

317. Nancy Collier. Born 1835. Died ? .

318. Didama Collier. Born 1836. Died ? .

319. John Collier. Born 1840. Died ? .

320. David Collier. Born 1840. Died ? .

321. William Collier. Born 1842. Died ? .

322. Elizabeth Collier. Born 1844. Died ? .

323. McMullin Collier. Born 1846. Died ? .

324. Mahala Ann Collier. Born 1848. Died ? .

325. Isaac Witt. Born 1838 in Kentucky. Died 1889.

Information about the marriage and children is from Laningham and Lombardo.

He married Mary Ann "Polly" Clarkston, daughter of James Clarkston & Mary Morris, 24 Aug 1864 in Harlan County, KY. Born ? . Died ? . They had the following children:

547	i.	James H. Witt
548	ii.	Archibald Witt
549	iii.	Henry T. Witt
550	iv.	Edmund Witt
551	v.	John Silas Witt
552	vi.	Martha Jane Witt
553	vii.	Mary Ann Witt
554	viii.	General Marion Witt
555	ix.	Elvada Witt

326. Edmond Witt. Born 1839 in Harlan County, KY. Died ? .

Information about the wife and children is from Laningham and Lombardo.

He married Louise "Eliza" Clarkston, daughter of James Clarkston & Mary Morris, 9 Mar 1864. Born ? . Died ? . They had the following children:

556	i.	Celia A. Witt
557	ii.	Mary E. Witt
558	iii.	Isaac N. V. Witt
559	iv.	Daniel Witt

327. Anna Witt. Born 1842 in Kentucky. Died ? .

She married James Short. Born ? . Died ? (Laningham).

328. Cynthia Witt. Born 1843 in Kentucky. Died ? .

She married Absalom Huff, 23 Dec 1869 in Harlan County, KY. Born ? Died ? (Laningham).

329. John Witt. Born 1846 in Kentucky. Died 1 Oct 1855 in Lee County, VA.

330. Martha Witt. Born 1848 in Russell County, VA. Died ? .

She married Samuel Shepherd. Born ? . Died ? (Laningham).

331. Emeline Witt. Born 1851. Died Oct 1855 in Lee County, VA.

332. Mary Witt. Born 1854. Died 15 Aug 1855 in Lee County, VA.

333. Andrew Jackson Witt. Born Circa 1846. Died ? .

334. Wiley M. Witt. Born 1848. Died ? .

He married H. Johnson, 14 Aug 1872 in Lee County, VA. Born ? . Died ? (Lombardo).

335. Latticia Witt. Born 1850. Died ? .

336. Ambrose Witt. Born 19 Jun 1854 in Lee County, VA. Died 26 Oct 1926.

Information about the marriage and child is from Lombardo.

He married Alzira Octavia Davis, daughter of Eli Davis & Nancy Jones, 2 Jun 1880 in Lee County, VA. Born ? . Died ? . They had the following children:

    560   i.   Flora Grace Witt

337. James D. Witt. Born Circa 1854. Died ? .

338. Eli Witt. Born 18 Feb 1858. Died ? .

339. Martha Witt. Born 19 Jun 1860. Died ? .

340. Robert Witt. Born Circa 1862. Died ? .

341. Nancy Witt. Born Circa 1863. Died ? .

342. Mary Witt. Born Circa 1864. Died ? .

343. Sarah Francis Witt. Born 10 Apr 1869. Died ? .

344. Cynthia Witt. Born 1873. Died 20 Aug 1885.

345. Ira G. Witt. Born 1875. Died ? .

346. Nellie C. Witt. Born Apr 1879. Died ? .

347. Jacob Witt. Born 1844. Died 10 Mar 1893 in Lee County, VA.

348. Prissa Witt. Born 1846. Died ? .

349. Archable Witt. Born 1848. Died ? .

350. Elizabeth Witt. Born 1850. Died ? .

351. James Witt. Born 1852. Died ? .

352. Lavinia J. Witt. Born 1854. Died ? .

353. Andrew Witt. Born 1857. Died ? .

354. William Witt. Born 1858. Died ? .

355. Edward Witt. Born ? . Died ? .

He married Mary Eldridge, 9 Feb 1871 in Lee County, VA. Born ? . Died ? (Lombardo).

356. Nancy Witt. Born Circa 1852. Died ? .

357. Elizabeth Witt. Born Jul 1852 in Virginia. Died ? .

Information about the marriage and children is from Lombardo.

She married Hampton Short, 1 Mar 1873 in Harlan County, KY. Born ? . Died ? . They had the following children:

561	i.	Charley Short
562	ii.	Mary Short
563	iii.	Hampton Short Jr.
564	iv.	Sarah J. Short
565	v.	Rozella Short
566	vi.	Lily Victoria Short
567	vii.	James Short

358. Emeline Witt. Born 1854. Died ? .

359. Rebecca Witt. Born 1856. Died ? .

360. Mary Ann Witt. Born 14 Sep 1859 in Lee County, VA. Died 3 Jul 1926 in Clay County, KY.

She first married Wright Short, After 1879. Born ? . Died ? (Lombardo).

She second married William Bowling, 1918. Born ? . Died ? (Lombardo).

361. John Witt. Born Feb 1864 in Russell County, VA. Died ? .

According to Lombardo, John and Rebecca had children but were not married; Louisa and Rosa were his wives.

He first married Louisa Parker, daughter of John Parker & Sarah Caudill, 1882 in Harlan County, KY. Born 1865. Died ? . They had the following children:

568	i.	Andrew Jackson Witt
569	ii.	John Wesley Witt
570	iii.	Roza B. Witt
571	iv.	Garfield Witt
572	v.	Leman Witt
573	vi.	Mary Witt
574	vii.	Tommy Witt

He did not marry Rebecca Parker, daughter of John Parker & Sarah Caudill. Born ? . Died ? . They had the following children:

575	i.	Mindy Witt (Illegitimate)
576	ii.	Alex Witt (Illegitimate)
577	iii.	Sarah Mandy Witt (Illegitimate)
578	iv.	Rachel Witt (Illegitimate)
579	v.	Robert Witt (Illegitimate)

He second married Rosa Parsons, 11 Aug 1909 in Harlan County, KY. Born ? . Died ? . They had the following children:

580	i.	Hubert Witt
581	ii.	Mendy Witt
582	iii.	Maude Witt
583	iv.	Fannie Witt
584	v.	Delmas Witt
585	vi.	Bessie Witt
586	vii.	James Witt

362. Charles Witt. Born Feb 1870. Died ? .

363. Anderson Witt. Born 1811 in Jefferson County, TN. Died After 1880.

All information is from Gendex.

He married Sarah Parmer, 10 Nov 1831 in Knox County, TN. Born ? . Died ? . They had the following children:

587	i.	Noah H. Witt
588	ii.	Nancy A. Witt
589	iii.	Leonard H. Witt
590	iv.	Sarah Elizabeth Witt

364. Jane Witt. Born 6 Jun 1802. Died ? .

She married Jesse Shirley, 22 Jan 1823. Born ? . Died ? (Gorin, *Bible and Family Records*, 315).

365. Polly Witt. Born 20 Jun 1804. Died 15 Apr 1849.

366. Elizabeth Witt. Born 20 May 1806. Died ? .

She married William Booth. Born ? . Died ? (Gorin, *Bible and Family Records*, 315).

367. Nancy Witt. Born 23 Mar 1808. Died ? .

Charles refers to Nancy in his will as Nancy Lain (Gorin, *Will Book 3*, 121). I have found no Lain/Lane in the Barren County Census for 1850 with a wife named Nancy who is the appropriate age.

She married ? Lain. Born ? . Died ? .

368. Jarusha Witt. Born 4 Feb 1810. Died 10 Nov 1849.

369. John Witt. Born 19 Nov 1811. Died ? .

Information about the wife and children is from the Barren County, KY, Census for 1860.

He married Unis M. ?. Born ? . Died ? . They had the following children:

591	i.	William L. Witt
592	ii.	Benjamin F. Witt
593	iii.	Emily J. Witt
594	iv.	Lucy M. Witt
595	v.	Mary E. Witt
596	vi.	Nancy A. Witt
597	vii.	Alice G. Witt

370. William Logan Witt. Born 21 Feb 1814. Died Oct 1824.

371. Benjamin F. Witt. Born 29 Feb 1816. Died Oct 1824.

372. Unnamed Witt. Born ? . Died ? .

373. Julia Ann Witt. Born 15 Apr 1818. Died ? .

Charles refers to Julia in his will as Julia Lain (Gorin, *Will Book 3*, 122). There is no Lain in the 1850 Barren County Census, but there is a Samuel Lane with wife Julia A., whose age is given as 34; in the 1860 Census Julia's age is 42, which would be the correct age for Julia Witt. I have no other confirmation, though, that this Julia A. is Charles Witt's Julia Ann. The information about the children is also from the Census for 1850 and 1860.

She married Samuel Lain. Born Circa 1809. Died ? . They had the following children:

598	i.	Frances C. Lain
599	ii.	John W. Lain
600	iii.	Mary A. Lain
601	iv.	Charles J. Lain
602	v.	C. Cissa Lain
603	vi.	Jo M. Lain
604	vii.	Ben W. Lain

374. Unnamed Witt. Born ? . Died ? .

375. Charles Foster Witt. Born 16 Nov 1821. Died ? .

He married Malinda Cummins, Circa 1850. Born ? . Died ? (Gorin, *Marriages of Barren County,* 74).

376. Andrew Jackson Witt. Born 2 Jul 1824. Died ? .

He married Margaret Minton, 1853. Born ? . Died ? (Gorin, *Marriages of Barren County*, 74).

377. Catherine H. Witt. Born 5 Jan 1827. Died 29 Aug 1848.

378. Emily M. Witt. Born 29 Aug 1829. Died 6 Apr 1850.

379. Amelia Witt. Born 8 Jan 1837. Died ? .

380. Sarah Witt. Born 11 Dec 1841. Died ? .

381. David William Witt. Born 11 Apr 1843. Died ? .

382. John R. Witt. Born 20 Jun 1845. Died ? .

383. Lucy Ellen Witt. Born 10 Nov 1847. Died ? .

She married George W. Tisdale, in Kentucky. Born ? . Died ? (Norton).

384. Eliza Witt. Born 27 Feb 1850. Died ? .

385. Fannie Witt. Born 14 Jan 1852. Died ? .

386. Alice Witt. Born 29 Feb 1856. Died ? .

387. Mary Witt. Born 30 Dec 1859. Died ? .

388. Mateson M. Witt. Born 1829. Died ? .

He married Minerva ?, About 1854. Born 1826. Died ? . They had the following children:

    605   i.   John Witt

389. Adoline Witt. Born 1831. Died ? .

390. Jerimah Witt. Born 1834. Died ? .

391. Mary Witt. Born 1836. Died ? .

392. Elizabeth Witt. Born 1838. Died ? .

393. Ginna Witt. Born 1840. Died ? .

394. Allen Witt. Born 1843. Died ? .

395. John Witt. Born 1846. Died ? .

396. Ellen Witt. Born 1848. Died ? .

397. Jesse Pendergrass Jr. Born Circa 1843 in Tennessee. Died ? .

398. Charles L. Witt. Born 1852. Died ? .

399. Sarah A. Witt. Born 1851. Died ? .

400. Mary A. Witt. Born 1858. Died ? .

401. James Witt. Born 1838. Died ? .

402. Alabama Witt. Born 1840. Died ? .

403. Charles Witt. Born 1842. Died ? .

404. Mary Witt. Born 1843. Died ? .

405. Samuel Witt. Born 1845. Died ? .

406. Almyra Witt. Born 1847. Died ? .

407. John Witt. Born 1850. Died ? .

408. Nancy Ann Varner. Born ? . Died ? .

She married Return Brown. Born ? . Died ? .

409. James J. Varner. Born ? . Died ? .

410. Mary Alabama Varner. Born ? . Died ? .

She first married William Clift Wallace. Born ? . Died ? .

She second married William Graham. Born ? . Died ? .

411. Sarah Varner. Born ? . Died ? .

She married W K Gray. Born ? . Died ? .

412. John Varner. Born ? . Died ? .

413. Ester Varner. Born ? . Died ? .

414. Sophronia Varner. Born ? . Died ? .

415. Elizabeth Varner. Born ? . Died ? .

416. Mary A. Witt. Born 23 Mar 1843 in Tennessee. Died 8 Apr 1913 in Taylor County, KY. Buried in Union Ridge Cemetery.

She married William E. Bookout. Born 4 Oct 1830 in Tennessee. Died 18 Nov 1902 in Taylor County, KY. Buried in Union Ridge Cemetery. They had the following children:

606	i.	B. Della Bookout
607	ii.	Laura J. Bookout
608	iii.	Lavina A. Bookout

417. Adolphus (Dof) Witt. Born Circa 1844 in Tennessee. Died ? .

Adolphus may have been called Doc; if so he moved to Mansville.

418. Maria E. Witt. Born 1845 in Tennessee. Died ? .

The E may have been Emily. She married John Calvin Bookout. Born Circa 1835. Died ? . They had the following children:

609	i.	Tennessee Jane Bookout
610	ii.	Mary Allie Bookout
611	iii.	William Edgar Bookout

419. Elizabeth B. Witt. Born 1846 in Hamilton County, TN. Died Before 1860.

420. James D. Witt. Born 14 Apr 1847 in Maryville, Blount County, TN. Died 20 Oct 1902 in Casey County, KY.

He married Sarah E. Bell, 11 Mar 1866 in Liberty, KY. Born 1 Dec 1844 in Casey County, KY. Died 31 Jan 1936 in Casey County, KY. They had the following children:

612	i.	Marietta Witt
613	ii.	Samuel Joseph Witt
614	iii.	Charles Sherman Witt
615	iv.	William E. (Willie) Witt
616	v.	Eliza J. Witt
617	vi.	Ulysses S. (Babe) Witt
618	vii.	Laura Witt
619	viii.	James Callie Witt
620	ix.	Welby Witt
621	x.	Matilda (Tillie) Witt
622	xi.	Celeste Witt
623	xii.	Lora Witt
624	xiii.	Infant

421. Chelf Witt. Born Circa 1850 in Tennessee. Died ? .

422. Melissa A. Witt. Born Apr 1852 in Chattanooga, TN. Died 1941.

She married William A. Chelf, 21 Nov 1872 in Taylor County, KY. Born 26 Jul 1850. Died 27 Aug 1876. They had the following children:

625	i.	Oschar A. Chelf
626	ii.	Loretha O. Chelf

423. Charles Lewis Witt. Born 1854 in Overton County, TN. Died 1941 in Campbellsville, KY. Buried in Union Ridge Cemetery.

Charles acquired a great deal of land. He married Mildred S. Puryear, 2 Aug 1877 in Taylor County, KY. Born 1854 in Taylor County, KY. Died 1919 in Campbellsville, KY. Buried in Union Ridge Cemetery. They had the following children:

627	i.	Flora Bell Witt

424. Wesley Randolph Witt. Born 13 May 1857 in Tennessee. Died 10 Oct 1930 in Taylor County, KY. Buried in Union Ridge Cemetery.

He married Emily C. Puryear. Born 14 Apr 1855. Died 28 Dec 1907 in Taylor County, KY. Buried in Union Ridge Cemetery. They had the following children:

628	i.	Harold Witt
629	ii.	? Witt
630	iii.	Nell Witt
631	iv.	Jesse Witt
632	v.	Parker Witt

425. Vestina A. Witt. Born 8 Oct 1859 in Fentress County, TN. Died ? .

She married Thomas T. Fisher, 9 Jul 1879 in Taylor County, KY. Born 28 May 1842. Died ? . They had the following children:

633	i.	Eva O. Fisher
634	ii.	Leah Nora Fisher
635	iii.	Stella A. Fisher
636	iv.	? Fisher
637	v.	Virginia Fisher
638	vi.	T. T. Fisher

426. Victoria Witt. Born Circa 1860 in Tennessee. Died ? .

She married William Bookout. Born ? . Died ? .

427. Emily (?) Witt. Born ? . Died ? .

428. Eliza A Witt. Born 1844 in Fentriss County, TN. Died ? .

429. Sarah J. Witt. Born 1845 in Fentriss County, TN. Died ? .

430. John A. Witt. Born 1849 in Fentress County, TN. Died ? .

431. Mary E. Witt. Born 1854 in Fentriss County, TN. Died ? .

432. Martha C. Witt. Born 1856 in Fentress County, TN. Died ? .

433. Levina E. Witt. Born 1859 in Fentress County, TN. Died ? .

434. William Witt. Born ? . Died ? .

He married Victoria Godman. Born ? . Died ? (Graham).

435. Amanda Witt. Born ? . Died ? .

She married Joseph Nadeau. Born ? . Died ? (Graham).

436. James H. Witt. Born ? . Died ? .

James never married (Graham).

437. Rebecca Witt. Born ? . Died ? .

She married David Richardson. Born ? . Died ? (Graham).

438. Dean Witt. Born ? . Died ? .

She married Elihu Kirby. Born ? . Died ? (Graham).

439. John V. Witt. Born ? . Died ? .

John moved to Colorado (Graham).

440. Polly Ann Witt. Born ? . Died ? .

She married Jushua Amerine. Born ? . Died ? (Graham).

441. Jefferson Witt. Born ? . Died ? .

Jefferson went West (Graham).

442. Phoebe Ann Witt. Born ? . Died ? .

She married Henry White. Born ? . Died ? (Graham).

443. Cynthia Witt. Born 10 Nov 1838. Died ? .

444. William Witt. Born 20 Sep 1840. Died ? .

445. Clayborn Witt. Born 6 Jul 1842. Died ? .

446. Thomas Jefferson Witt. Born 25 Aug 1845. Died ? .

447. Isaiah Witt. Born 20 Jul 1846. Died ? .

448. David H. Witt. Born 9 May 1848. Died ? .

449. Nancy E. Witt. Born 20 Jan 1850 in Estill County, KY. Died 8 Jan 1889 in Osborne, MO.

Information about the marriage and children is from Gendex.

She married Edwin Frances Durbin, 10 Nov 1867 in Estill County, KY. Born ? . Died ? . They had the following children:

639	i.	James Bruce Durbin
640	ii.	Frances Durbin
641	iii.	Ada Durbin
642	iv.	Jesse Durbin
643	v.	Joseph Ambrose Durbin
644	vi.	Mary Emma Durbin
645	vii.	William Anthony Durbin
646	viii.	Rhoda May Durbin
647	ix.	Gibbon Durbin

450. John Witt. Born 26 May 1852. Died ? .

451. James M. Witt. Born 12 Mar 1854. Died ? .

452. Jesse Witt. Born 3 Mar 1857. Died ? .

453. Asa Witt. Born 26 Jan 1859.

454. Elizabeth Witt. Born 3 Mar 1862. Died ? .

455. John W. Witt. Born 11 Oct 1844. Died 23 Mar 1862.

456. George R. Witt. Born 5 May 1847. Died 6 Dec 1887.

457. Sarah L. Witt. Born 25 Jul 1850. Died 4 Jun 1853.

458. Benjamin J. Witt. Born 24 Nov 1852. Died 24 Nov 1860.

459. Hester Jane Witt. Born 11 Mar 1854. Died 18 Dec 1877.

460. David Nelson Witt. Born 7 Sep 1856. Died 10 Apr 1944.

Information about the wife and children is from Graham.

He married Emma Winburn. Born 21 Jun 1860. Died 6 May 1904. They had the following children:

648	i.	James William Witt

649	ii.	Hester Jane Witt
650	iii.	George H. Witt
651	iv.	Sarah Witt
652	v.	Carrie Witt
653	vi.	John Q. Witt
654	vii.	Owen O. Witt
655	viii.	Mayme Witt
656	ix.	Anna Pearl Witt
657	x.	Joe A. P. Witt
658	xi.	Robert Vernon Witt
659	xii.	Lee Ella Witt

461. Henry Clayton Witt. Born 31 May 1861. Died 12 Dec 1926.
Information about the marriage and children is from Graham.

He married Lousinda Burilla Witt, daughter of John M. Witt &
Emaline A. Jacobs. Born 11 Dec 1868. Died 11 Dec 1924. They had the
following children:

660	i.	Maud Ella Witt
661	ii.	Bessie Lee Witt
662	iii.	Gardner R. Witt
663	iv.	Earl Omer Witt
664	v.	Emma Jane Witt
665	vi.	Hattie Lenora Witt
666	vii.	Myrtle Witt
667	viii.	Rhoda Susan Witt
668	ix.	Ernest Yerkes Witt
669	x.	Leonard Raymond Witt
670	xi.	Lenna Clay Witt
671	xii.	Eugene Kennon Witt

462. Josepha Witt. Born ? . Died ? .
She married Adams Douglas Rev.. Born ? . Died ? (Graham).

463. Louvinia J. Witt. Born ? . Died ? .

She married George Witt. Born ? . Died ? (Graham).

464. Milda Witt. Born ? . Died ? .

She married Ben Witt. Born ? . Died ? (Graham).

465. Barthena Witt. Born ? . Died ? .

She married John S. Tuttle. Born ? . Died ? (Graham).

466. Sarah J. Witt. Born ? . Died ? .

She married Ben Kerr. Born ? . Died ? (Graham).

467. Francis Witt. Born ? . Died ? .

She married James Holman. Born ? . Died ? (Graham).

468. Ellen Witt. Born ? . Died ? .

She married John Kindred. Born ? . Died ? (Graham).

469. Louisa Ann Witt. Born ? . Died ? .

She married William Welburn. Born ? . Died ? (Graham).

470. McClellan Witt. Born ? . Died ? .

He married Virginia Walthers. Born ? . Died ? (Graham).

471. Emaline Witt. Born ? . Died ? .

She married Robert S. Harris. Born ? . Died ? (Graham).

472. William Witt. Born ? . Died ? .

He married Armanda Winburn. Born ? . Died ? (Graham).

473. Fannie Witt. Born ? . Died ? .

She married Newton Tuttle. Born ? . Died ? (Graham).

474. H. M. Witt. Born ? . Died ? .

He married Anna Harris. Born ? . Died ? (Graham).

475. Sarah Witt. Born ? . Died ? .

She married William Finney. Born ? . Died ? (Graham).

476. Delaney Witt Jr. Born ? . Died ? .

He married Nannie Vaughn. Born ? . Died ? (Graham).

477. Charley Witt. Born ? . Died ? .

He married Margit Groves. Born ? . Died ? (Graham).

478. **Clabe Witt.** Born ? . Died ? .

He married A. Wrinkler Loukett. Born ? . Died ? (Graham).

479. **Sarah Ella Witt.** Born 17 Oct 1859. Died 20 Jan 1911.

She married William N. Gould. Born ? . Died ? (Graham).

480. **Issac N. Witt.** Born 17 Apr 1862. Died ? .

He married Susa E. Gooch. Born ? . Died ? (Graham).

481. **William L. Witt.** Born 10 Sep 1866. Died 21 May 1939.

He married Nannie S. Cockrill. Born ? . Died ? (Graham).

482. **Lousinda Burilla Witt.** Born 11 Dec 1868. Died 11 Dec 1924.

Information about the marriage and children is from Graham.

She married Henry Clayton Witt, son of James Witt & Lavinia Jane Dunaway. Born 31 May 1861. Died 12 Dec 1926. They had the following children:

660	i.	Maud Ella Witt
661	ii.	Bessie Lee Witt
662	iii.	Gardner R. Witt
663	iv.	Earl Omer Witt
664	v.	Emma Jane Witt
665	vi.	Hattie Lenora Witt
666	vii.	Myrtle Witt
667	viii.	Rhoda Susan Witt
668	ix.	Ernest Yerkes Witt
669	x.	Leonard Raymond Witt
670	xi.	Lenna Clay Witt
671	xii.	Eugene Kennon Witt

483. **Eugene Witt.** Born 17 Apr 1873. Died 8 Sep 1928.

He married Myrtle Bybee, 30 Jan 1904. Born ? . Died 17 Jul 1960 (Graham).

484. **Asa William Witt.** Born ? . Died ? .

Information about the marriage and children is from Norton.

He married Susan Tucker McAlexander. Born ? . Died 1910.

They had the following children:

    672   i.   Malie Emma Witt

    673   ii.   Susan Bell Witt

    674   iii.   William Asa Witt

    675   iv.   Joseph Henry Witt

    676   v.   Melville Lee Witt

485. Jesse David Witt. Born ? . Died ? .

Information about the marriage and child is from Norton.

He married Nancy Strickland. Born ? . Died ? . They had the following children:

    677   i.   Alonzo K. Witt

486. Dennet Abner Witt. Born 1843. Died 1882.

Information about the marriage and children is from Norton.

He married Elizabeth McComb. Born ? . Died ? . They had the following children:

    678   i.   John W. Witt

    679   ii.   Allie Witt

    680   iii.   Silvie Witt

    681   iv.   Elizabeth Witt

    682   v.   Woods Witt

    683   vi.   Mack Witt

    684   vii.   Sadie Witt

    685   viii. Mattie Witt

487. John Witt. Born ? . Died ? .

Information about the marriage and children is from Norton.

He married Sarah Loving. Born ? . Died ? . They had the following children:

    686   i.   Robert Witt

    687   ii.   Clinton Witt

    688   iii.   Charlie Witt

    689   iv.   Hattie Witt

690   v.   Margaret Witt

488. Sallie Witt. Born ? . Died ? .

Information about the marriage and children is from Norton.

She married Dier Martin. Born ? . Died ? . They had the following children:

691   i.   Lucy Martin

692   ii.   Dicie Martin

693   iii.   Mildred Martin

694   iv.   Nancy Martin

695   v.   Constance Martin

489. Connie Witt. Born ? . Died ? .

She married Terry Baily. Born ? . Died ? (Norton).

490. Nanny Witt. Born ? . Died ? .

Norton has the same husband for Connie and Nanny.

She married Terry Baily. Born ? . Died ? .

491. John Hatcher. Born ? . Died ? .

492. Lavinia Hatcher. Born ? . Died ? .

493. Hilery Hatcher. Born ? . Died ? .

494. Abner Hatcher. Born ? . Died ? .

495. William E. Witt. Born 23 Mar 1840. Died ? .

He married Laura L. Bruce. Born ? . Died ? (Norton).

496. David H. Witt. Born 1 Apr 1842. Died ? .

David never married (Norton).

497. Robert R. Witt. Born 17 Jul 1851. Died ? .

He married Maggie N. Williams, 20 Apr 1876. Born ? . Died ? (Norton).

498. Bettie D. Witt. Born 25 Apr 1854 in Roanoke, VA. Died ? .

She married Robert S. McCleur, 31 Oct 1876. Born ? . Died ? (Norton).

499. Laminia Witt. Born 3 Mar 1857. Died ? .

She married E. B. Wilson, 20 Dec 1882. Born ? . Died ?

(Norton).

500. Charlie M. Witt. Born 19 Sep 1859. Died 1918 in Fresno, CA.

501. George D. Witt. Born ? . Died ? .

He married Dora L. Wade, 4 Dec 1877 in Lynchburg, VA. Born ? . Died ? (Norton).

502. Charles Witt. Born ? . Died ? .

503. Thomas Witt. Born ? . Died ? .

504. John Witt. Born ? . Died ? .

505. Sallie Witt. Born ? . Died ? .

She married Robert Tinsley. Born ? . Died ? (Norton).

506. Martha Elizabeth F. Witt. Born 1837 in Nelson County, VA. Died ? .

She first married Samuel W. Hargis. Born Circa 1831 in TN. Died Before 1880 in Allen County, KY.

Samuel and Elizabeth are listed in the 1870 Census, but by 1880 Elizabeth is listed with William Hood along with her two youngest children by Samuel. Isabella is a member of the household of James Witt, her grandfather. Samuel and Elizabeth had the following children:

696	i.	Isabella Hargis
697	ii.	Margaret F. Hargis
698	iii.	John D. Hargis
699	iv.	James L. Hargis
700	v.	Lula Hargis

She second married William M. Hood. Born Circa 1835. Died ? .

507. William H. Witt. Born 7 Feb 1840 in Allen County, KY. Died 19 Jan 1920 in Allen County, KY. Buried in Maynard, New Bethel Church Cemetery.

He married Mary J. Pruitt, daughter of Robin Pruitt & Luna Stone, 9 Aug 1865 in Allen County, KY. Born 15 Mar 1841. Died 5 Feb 1920 in Allen County, KY. Buried in Maynard, New Bethel Church Cemetery. They had the following children:

701	i.	Lawretta Witt
702	ii.	William H. Witt Jr.
703	iii.	George W. Witt
704	iv.	John Witt
705	v.	James F. Witt

508. Sidney W. Witt. Born 2 Jan 1842 in Allen County, KY. Died 20 Mar 1922 in Allen County, KY. Buried in Maynard, New Bethel Church Cemetery.

In James's will Sidney was given the tract of land he was living on and deeded more land by William H. after James's death. Sidney enlisted in Private Company E 52nd Regiment Kentucky Mounted Infantry in 1863 and served until the end of the war in 1865.

He married Sallie E. Williams, 5 Feb 1873 in Scottsville, KY. Born 12 Oct 1852. Died 3 May 1921 in Allen County, KY. Buried in Maynard, New Bethel Church Cemetery. They had the following children:

706	i.	James Letcher Witt
707	ii.	Henri Ella Witt
708	iii.	Elbridge Witt
709	iv.	Charles Lon Witt
710	v.	William Bertram Witt
711	vi.	Herschell H. Witt
712	vii.	Lula Witt
713	viii.	Bettie Witt

509. John F. Witt. Born 30 Nov 1846 in Allen County, KY. Died 5 Aug 1923 in Barren County, KY. Buried in Barren County, Austin Cemetery (Leech and Beard 12).

Sometime between 1870 and 1880 John and Eliza Belle moved to Barren County. Information about the marriage is from Barren County Marriage Records; information about the children is from Barren County Census Records.

He married Eliza Belle Berry. Born 25 Sep 1852. Died 12 Nov 1933 in Barren County, KY. Buried in Barren County, Austin Cemetery (Leech and Beard 12). They had the following children:

714	i.	Capernia Witt
715	ii.	William T. Witt
716	iii.	Nannie Witt
717	iv.	Robert E. Witt
718	v.	Lucy Witt
719	vi.	Laura Witt

510. Luther H. Witt. Born 22 Dec 1849 in Allen County, KY. Died 29 Dec 1942 in Monroe County, KY. Buried in Barren County, Pleasant Homes Church Cemetery.

Informaion about the children is from Barren County Census Records.

He married Caroline Franklin. Born 1851. Died ? . They had the following children:

720	i.	Oscar Grayson Witt
721	ii.	James E. Witt
722	iii.	Ora M. Witt
723	iv.	William F. Witt
724	v.	Lon P. Witt
725	vi.	Cecil Witt

511. Camden Hezikiah Witt. Born ? . Died ? .

Information about the marriage and children is from Norton.

He married Rochelle Simms. Born ? . Died ? . They had the following children:

726	i.	Eleanor G. Witt
727	ii.	Madie Witt
728	iii.	Daniel Witt

512. Daniel Kirk Witt. Born ? . Died ? .

Information about the marriage and children is from Norton.

He married Cora Baily. Born ? . Died ? . They had the following children:

729   i.   Gordon Burgess Witt

730   ii.   Maude Elizabeth Witt

731   iii.   Mary Kathleen Witt

732   iv.   Robert Hezikiah Witt

733   v.   Annie Kirk Witt

734   vi.   Margaret Brand Witt

735   vii.   William Randolph Witt

736   viii.   Virginia Hierbemont Witt

513. Florence Witt. Born ? . Died ? .

514. Josephine Cornelia Witt. Born ? . Died ? .
She married Samuel Robinson. Born ? . Died ? (Norton).

515. Candice (Dicie) Witt. Born ? . Died ? .

516. Roland Witt. Born Dec 1838. Died ? .
He married Elizabeth Collins. Born ? . Died ? (Norton).

517. Sarah Ann Witt. Born 18 Mar 1840. Died ? .
She married ? Beasley. Born ? . Died ? (Norton).

518. John M. Witt. Born ? . Died ? .
John moved to Arkansas (Norton).

519. Nancy Witt. Born Feb 1842. Died ? .
She married ? Eubank. Born ? . Died ? . Nancy and her husband moved to Fayette, Missouri (Norton).

520. Ella Dickenson. Born ? . Died ? .

521. Louise Dickenson. Born ? . Died ? .

522. Christie Dickenson. Born ? . Died ? .

523. Elizabeth Collins. Born ? . Died ? .

524. Addison Collins. Born ? . Died ? .

525. Samuel Collins. Born ? . Died ? .

526. John Collins. Born ? . Died ? .

527. Kizzie Ann Witt. Born Circa 1827 in Hamilton County, IL.

Died ? .

Information about the marriages is from Gendex.

She first married Ace Wood, Circa 1847. Born ? . Died ? .

She second married ? Hamilton, Circa 1850. Born ? . Died ? .

528. John Wesley Witt. Born 10 Feb 1829 in Hamilton County, IL. Died 30 Jun 1907 in Heber City, Utah.

Information about the marriages is from Gendex.

He first married Lavinia Bigelow, 27 Mar 1851 in Farmington, Utah. Born ? . Died ? .

He second married Martha Jane Taylor, 1 Nov 1869 in Heber City, Utah. Born ? . Died ? .

529. Sarah Jane Witt. Born 11 Feb 1831 in Hamilton County, IL. Died 31 Dec 1875 in Heber City, Utah. WASATCH

Information is from Gendex.

She married Elisha Averett, 19 Jan 1846 in Hancock County, IL. Born ? . Died ? . They had the following children:

737	i.	Dorcas Averett
738	ii.	Elisha Averett
739	iii.	Sarah Jane Averett
740	iv.	Kizzie Ann Averett
741	v.	John Harvey Averett
742	vi.	Elijah Averett
743	vii.	George Averett
744	viii.	Robert Wesley Averett
745	ix.	James Lafayette Averett
746	x.	Lucy Lavinia Averett
747	xi.	Jennette Eliza Averett
748	xii.	Byron Averett
749	xiii.	David Averett

530. William Witt. Born 1833 in Hamilton County, IL. Died Circa 1833 in Hamilton County, IL.

531. Miles Witt. Born 1834 in Hamilton County, IL. Died Circa 1834 in Hamilton County, IL.

532. Martha Jane Witt. Born ? . Died ? .

Information about the marriage and children is from Lombardo.

She married Marion Flanary, son of John Flanary & Sally Morris, 12 Aug 1887 in Lee County, VA. Born ? . Died ? . They had the following children:

750	i.	Charley Flanary
751	ii.	Susie Flanary
752	iii.	Vilder Flanary
753	iv.	Cornie Mae Flanary
754	v.	William E. Flanary
755	vi.	Sally Flanary
756	vii.	Corbin Flanary
757	viii.	Elsie Flanary

533. Alpha E. Witt. Born ? . Died ? .

She married William G. Banks, 31 Dec 1886 in Lee County, VA. Born ? . Died ? (Lombardo).

534. Docia Witt. Born ? . Died ? .

She married J. M. Bayless, 8 May 1887 in Lee County, VA. Born ? . Died ? (Lombardo).

535. Mary A. Witt. Born ? . Died ? .

She married E. M. Cooper, 18 Apr 1879 in Lee County, VA. Born ? . Died ? (Lombardo).

536. James M. Witt. Born 1859. Died Aug 1893 in Lee County, VA.

537. John B. Floyd Witt. Born 9 Feb 1862. Died ? .

Information about the wife and children is from Laningham (337-338).

He married Ellen Debusk, daughter of John Debusk. Born 11 Feb 1863 in Lee County, VA. Died ? . They had the following children:

758	i.	Andy Lee Witt

759	ii.	Ida J. Witt
760	iii.	Charles R. Witt
761	iv.	Edily Florence Witt
762	v.	Leonard L. Witt

538. John H. Witt. Born 27 Feb 1874. Died ? .

539. James Monroe Witt. Born 9 Feb 1877. Died 4 Sep 1954 in Taylor, MI.

540. Eliza Kate Witt. Born ? . Died ? .

Information about the husbands and child is from Laningham (337-338).

She first married Claude Allen. Born ? . Died ? . They had the following children:

| 763 | i. | Billie Allen Allen |

She second married A. W. Wagner. Born ? . Died ? .

After Eliza Kate divorced Claude Allen and married A. W. "Bud" Wagner, "Bud" adopted Billie Allen (Laningham).

541. Carrie E. Witt. Born 1 Apr 1886. Died ? .

She married Lawrence H. McWane. Born ? . Died ? (Laningham).

542. Roy M. Witt. Born 15 Jul 1888. Died ? .

543. Earnest Clyde Witt. Born 30 Mar 1890. Died ? .

544. Hazen Hurst Witt. Born Jun 1892. Died ? .

545. Infant Witt. Born Apr 1893. Died ? .

I do not know whether this child was male or female.

546. Edgar Kennedy Witt. Born 1 Apr 1893. Died ? .

547. James H. Witt. Born 22 Jun 1865 in Harlan County, KY. Died 1960 in Sarah, OK.

He married Matilda Mix, 1887. Born ? . Died ? (Lombardo).

548. Archibald Witt. Born 1867 in Harlan County, KY. Died Circa 1915 in Yell County, Arkansas.

He married Annis Hunt Flood. Born ? . Died ? (Lombardo).

549. Henry T. Witt. Born Circa 1869 in Harlan County, KY. Died ?
Henry never married (Lombardo).

550. Edmund Witt. Born Aug 1873 in Harlan County, KY. Died 28 Dec 1959 in Yell County, Arkansas.
He married Polly Hunt, 7 Oct 1905. Born ? . Died ? (Lombardo).

551. John Silas Witt. Born 9 Aug 1877 in Harlan County, KY. Died 7 Nov 1959 in Logan County, Arkansas.
He married Dodoa Ann Flood, 12 Aug 1894. Born ? . Died ? (Lombardo).

552. Martha Jane Witt. Born 1878 in Russell County, VA. Died 22 Dec 1932 in Antlers, OK.
She married James Henry Flood. Born ? . Died ? (Lombardo).

553. Mary Ann Witt. Born 1878. Died 1878.

554. General Marion Witt. Born 19 Aug 1881 in Leslie County, KY. Died 9 Mar 1973 in Yell County, Arkansas.

555. Elvada Witt. Born 1888 in Madison County, Arkansas. Died 22 Jul 1971 in Scottsdale, Arizona.
She married James Littleton, 4 Feb 1906. Born ? . Died ? (Lombardo).

556. Celia A. Witt. Born Circa 1865 in Harlan County, KY. Died ? .

557. Mary E. Witt. Born Circa 1867 in Harlan County, KY. Died ? .

558. Isaac N. V. Witt. Born Circa 1870 in Harlan County, KY. Died ? .

559. Daniel Witt. Born Circa 1879 in Harlan County, KY. Died 31 Jan 1940. Buried in Scott County, Arkansas.

560. Flora Grace Witt. Born 16 Oct 1887 in Lee County, VA. Died ? .

Information about the marriage and children is from Lombardo.

She married Hiram Leroy Brockman, 24 Dec 1918 in Norman, OK. Born ? . Died ? . They had the following children:

764	i.	Hiram Leroy Brockman Jr.
765	ii.	David Dean Brockman
766	iii.	Betty Lou Brockman

561. Charley Short. Born Mar 1879. Died ? .

562. Mary Short. Born Apr 1882 in Kentucky. Died ? .

Information about the husband and children is from Lombardo.

She married Bill Huff, 1900 in Harlan County, KY. Born ? .

They had the following children:

| 767 | i. | Cassie Huff |
| 768 | ii. | Ferrell Huff |

563. Hampton Short Jr. Born Mar 1885. Died ? .

564. Sarah J. Short. Born Feb 1887. Died ? .

Information about the husband and child is from Lombardo.

She married Ballard Kelly. Born ? . They had the following children:

| 769 | i. | Ballard Kelly Jr. |

565. Rozella Short. Born May 1889. Died ? .

She married Cy Kelly. Born ? . Died ? (Lombardo).

566. Lily Victoria Short. Born Jun 1890 in Harlan County, KY. Died ? .

Information about the husband and children is from Lombardo.

She married Wiley Holmes, 1910 in Harlan County, KY. Born ? . They had the following children:

770	i.	Flossie Holmes
771	ii.	Glenda Holmes
772	iii.	Edgar Holmes
773	iv.	Wilmer Holmes
774	v.	Delonia Holmes
775	vi.	Celia Holmes
776	vii.	Lana Holmes
777	viii.	Kermit Holmes

778   ix.   Comrad Holmes

567. James Short. Born ? . Died ? .

568. Andrew Jackson Witt. Born 8 Nov 1885 in Harlan, KY. Died Feb 1984 in London, KY. Buried in Sargant Cemetery, London, KY.

Information about the wife and children is from Lombardo.

He married Elizabeth Crider, daughter of Carter Crider & Mary Day, 26 Apr 1906 in Harlan, KY. Born 10 Oct 1888 in Harlan, KY. Died 21 Feb 1974 in London, KY. Buried in Sargant Cemetery, London, KY. They had the following children:

779   i.   Bertha M. Witt
780   ii.   Dillard Witt
781   iii.   Rushia Witt
782   iv.   Grant Witt
783   v.   Fred Witt
784   vi.   Newton Witt
785   vii.   Earl Witt
786   viii.   Ruby Witt
787   ix.   Verlia Opal Witt
788   x.   John Carter Witt
789   xi.   Harlen Ray Witt

569. John Wesley Witt. Born 28 Nov 1888. Died Mar 1977 in Holmes Mill, KY.

Information about the wife and children is from Lombardo.

He married Mary Doss, daughter of Steve Doss & America Smith. Born ? . Died ? . They had the following children:

790   i.   Howard Witt
791   ii.   Chester Witt
792   iii.   Lawrence Witt
793   iv.   Otis Witt
794   v.   Clercia Witt
795   vi.   Vilder Witt

796	vii.	Earl Edmond Witt
797	viii.	Beulah Witt
798	ix.	Ada Witt
799	x.	Geneva Charity Witt
800	xi.	Orcia Witt

570. Roza B. Witt. Born Nov 1893. Died ? .

571. Garfield Witt. Born Sep 1894. Died Sep 1970 in Harlan County, KY.

Information about the wife and children is from Lombardo.

He married Sarah Kelly, daughter of J. Kelly, 4 Jun 1915 in Harlan County, KY. Born ? . They had the following children:

801	i.	Oakie Witt
802	ii.	Alpha Witt

572. Leman Witt. Born 1898. Died ? .

573. Mary Witt. Born Mar 1899. Died ? .

574. Tommy Witt. Born 28 Mar 1905. Died Feb 1993 in Harlan County, KY.

Information about the wife and child is from Lombardo.

He married Minnie Creech. Born ? . Died ? . They had the following children:

803	i.	Sue Witt

575. Mindy Witt. Born 1879. Died ? .

576. Alex Witt. Born 1888. Died 19 Jul 1965 in Harlan County, KY.

He married Rosie Creech, 1910 in Harlan County, KY. Born ? . Died ? (Laningham).

577. Sarah Mandy Witt. Born Apr 1894. Died ? .

578. Rachel Witt. Born Mar 1897. Died ? .

Information about the husband and child is from Lombardo.

She married Billy King. Born ? . They had the following children:

804	i.	Hazel King

579. Robert Witt. Born 10 Jul 1904. Died May 1967.

Information about the wife and child is from Laningham.

He married Flora Kelly, 1923 in Harlan County, KY. Born ? .

Died ? . They had the following children:

    805   i.   Nora Witt

580. Hubert Witt. Born ? . Died ? .

He married Nora Blair, daughter of Paris Blair & Candis Short.

Born ? . They had the following children:

    806   i.   Alton Witt

    807   ii.   Louise Witt

    808   iii.   Sandra Witt

    809   iv.   Gwen Witt

581. Mendy Witt. Born ? . Died ? .

582. Maude Witt. Born 1910.

She married Ed McFarlan. Born ? (Lombardo).

583. Fannie Witt. Born 1913.

She married Curtis Rivers. Born ? (Lombardo).

584. Delmas Witt. Born 1915.

585. Bessie Witt. Born 1915.

She married Truman Rutherford, 17 May 1927 in Lee County,

VA. Born ? (Lombardo).

586. James Witt. Born 1917.

587. Noah H. Witt. Born 1832. Died ? .

588. Nancy A. Witt. Born 1836. Died ? .

She married William Chaney, 5 Dec 1858. Born ? . Died ? (Gendex).

589. Leonard H. Witt. Born 1839. Died 16 Mar 1902.

590. Sarah Elizabeth Witt. Born May 1842. Died ? .

Information about the marriage and children is from Gendex.

She married Elisha Albert Frank, 1 Dec 1861 in Jefferson County, TN. Born ? . Died ? . They had the following children:

    810   i.   John Elbert Frank

    811   ii.   William Anderson Frank

591. William L. Witt. Born 23 Oct 1842. Died 10 Dec 1865. Buried in Witt Cemetery, Barren County, KY.

Information about William's birth, death, and burial is from Leech and Beard (518).

592. Benjamin F. Witt. Born 1845. Died ? .

593. Emily J. Witt. Born 1848. Died ? .

594. Lucy M. Witt. Born 1850. Died ? .

595. Mary E. Witt. Born 1852. Died ? .

596. Nancy A. Witt. Born 1854. Died ? .

597. Alice G. Witt. Born 10 Apr 1857. Died 8 Jul 1858. Buried in Witt Cemetery, Barren County, KY.

Information about Alice's birth, death, and burial is from Leech and Beard (518).

598. Frances C. Lain. Born 1839. Died ? .

599. John W. Lain. Born 1841. Died ? .

600. Mary A. Lain. Born 1844. Died ? .

601. Charles J. Lain. Born 1846. Died ? .

602. C. Cissa Lain. Born 1848. Died ? .

603. Jo M. Lain. Born 1857. Died ? .

604. Ben W. Lain. Born 1860. Died ? .

605. John Witt. Born 1857. Died ? .

606. B. Della Bookout. Born 4 Aug 1880. Died 13 Mar 1900.

607. Laura J. Bookout. Born Circa 1866 in Taylor County, KY. Died ? .

608. Lavina A. Bookout. Born Circa 1870 in Taylor County, KY. Died ? .

609. Tennessee Jane Bookout. Born Circa 1866. Died ? .

610. Mary Allie Bookout. Born Circa 1869. Died ? .

611. William Edgar Bookout. Born ? . Died ? .

612. Marietta Witt. Born ? . Died 30 Nov 1889.

613. Samuel Joseph Witt. Born 24 Jan 1867 in Liberty, KY. Died 9 Jan 1937 in Liberty, KY. Buried in Fair Cemetery.

He first married Elizabeth B. (Lizzie) Henson, 9 Dec 1909 in Jeffersonville, IN. Born 13 May 1883. Died About 6 Nov 1967. Buried in Fair Cemetery.

Elizabeth was sometimes identified with the surname of Hughes. They had the following children:

812	i.	Ruth Witt
813	ii.	Ruby Witt
814	iii.	Samuel Joseph Witt Jr.

He second married Sarah M. (Sallie) Bell, 10 Feb 1890 in Casey County, KY. Born 2 Dec 1871 in Casey County, KY. Died 11 Aug 1908. Buried in Fair Cemetery. They had the following children:

815	i.	Arthur Witt
816	ii.	Otha Witt
817	iii.	Leslie Green Witt
818	iv.	Virgil A. Witt

819	v.	Curtis Witt
820	vi.	Herman Witt
821	vii.	Clyde Witt
822	viii.	James Witt

614. Charles Sherman Witt. Born 27 Jan 1870. Died 14 Jun 1936 in Liberty, KY.

He first married Mary Bell Hansford, 23 Jan 1890 in Casey County, KY. Born 1865 in Danville, KY. Died 1934. Buried in Fair Cemetery. They were divorced. They had the following children:

823	i.	Edgar Witt
824	ii.	Luther Witt
825	iii.	Oscar Witt
826	iv.	Della Witt
827	v.	Sally E. Witt

He second married Sally Mason, 20 May 1911. Born 1874. Died 1955.

Sherman Witt, Welby Baldock, and Willie Witt (Sherman's brother) were riding in a big truck when Sherman fell out and the truck ran over him. Some people speculated that Welby may have helped Sherman out the door in order to be with Sally, with whom he spent a lot of time after the funeral. Welby was supposed to be Sherman's best friend.

615. William E. (Willie) Witt. Born 15 Aug 1874. Died 1937 in Liberty, KY. Buried in Salem U.M. Church Cemetery.

He married Polly Payne, 15 Aug 1894. Born 1879. Died 1945. They had the following children:

828	i.	Alnier Witt
829	ii.	Ada Witt
830	iii.	Albert Witt
831	iv.	Claude Witt
832	v.	Ethel Witt

833	vi.	Almer Witt
834	vii.	Myrtle Witt
835	viii.	Stanley Pete Witt
836	ix.	Adell Witt
837	x.	Mildred Witt
838	xi.	Lorene Witt
839	xii.	Charles Witt

616. Eliza J. Witt. Born 23 Oct 1874. Died 23 Oct 1874 in Casey County, KY.

617. Ulysses S. (Babe) Witt. Born 23 Oct 1875 in Casey County, KY. Died 26 Jul 1965.

He first married Paschel E. Lucy Evans, 4 Dec 1902 in Casey County, KY. Born 1 Mar 1883. Died 20 Jul 1907 in Casey County, KY. Buried in Fair Cemetery. Paschel Lucy died during the birth of her second child. They had the following children:

| 840 | i. | Earl Witt |
| 841 | ii. | Audrey Witt |

He second married Rachel E. McDonald, 21 Feb 1915. Born 1894. Died 16 Apr 1992. They had the following children:

| 842 | i. | Beulah Witt |
| 843 | ii. | UNNAMED |

618. Laura Witt. Born 2 May 1877. Died 31 Mar 1900 in Liberty, KY. Buried in Walnut Hill Cemetery.

She married William Evans, 5 Dec 1894. Born Circa 1872. Died ? . They had the following children:

| 844 | i. | Jack Evans |

619. James Callie Witt. Born 28 Feb 1880. Died 13 Feb 1920. Buried in Antioch Cemetery.

He married Grace Hammonds. Born Circa 1885. Died ? . They had the following children:

| 845 | i. | Georgia Fay Witt |

620. Welby Witt. Born 28 Feb 1882 in Liberty, KY. Died 1969. Buried in Antioch Cemetery.

He married Myrtle M. (Ella) Baldock, 27 Dec 1910. Born 1888. Died 1969. They had the following children:

846	i.	Lucy Fay Witt
847	ii.	Lillian Witt
848	iii.	Forest Witt
849	iv.	Elizabeth Witt
850	v.	Kathlene Witt
851	vi.	Lillie May Witt

621. Matilda (Tillie) Witt. Born 6 Mar 1884. Died ? in New Castle, IN (?).

She first married ? Rea. Born ? . Died ? . They had the following children:

852	i.	Unnamed

She second married Ora Ellis, 1 Feb 1906. Born ? . Died ? .

622. Celeste Witt. Born 9 Oct 1886. Died Circa 1955. Buried in Ohio.

She married Add Ellis. Born Circa 1881. Died ? . They had the following children:

853	i.	Carl Ellis
854	ii.	Margie Ellis
855	iii.	Virgie (Virginia) Ellis
856	iv.	Adopted

623. Lora Witt. Born 29 Nov 1889. Died Circa 1940.

She married Clell Crockett, 15 Sep 1915. Born Circa 1884. Died ? in Greenwood, IN. They had the following children:

857	i.	Helen Patricia Crockett

624. Infant. Born 1890. Died ? .

625. Oschar A. Chelf. Born Apr 1874. Died 1939.

626. Loretha O. Chelf. Born Aug 1876 in Taylor County, KY. Died Mar 1877 in Taylor County, KY.

Loretha died of consumption.

627. Flora Bell Witt. Born 13 Nov 1881 in Taylor County, KY. Died 1967.

She married Clem Hill. Born ? . Died ? . They had the following children:

858	i.	Charles Marvin Hill
859	ii.	Lucille Hill
860	iii.	Ruby Hill
861	iv.	Carl Hill
862	v.	Edmonston Hill
863	vi.	Clementine Hill
864	vii.	Muriel Hill
865	viii.	Dorotha Hill
866	ix.	Jack Hill

628. Harold Witt. Born 20 Aug 1882. Died 20 Aug 1882. Buried in Union Ridge Cemetery.

629. ? Witt. Born Circa 1884. Died ? .

630. Nell Witt. Born Circa 1886. Died ? .

631. Jesse Witt. Born Circa 1888. Died ? .

She married Ray Herron. Born ? . Died ? . They had the following children:

867	i.	Catherine Herron
868	ii.	Chester Herron

632. Parker Witt. Born ? . Died ? in California.

Parker worked as a telegraph operator for the railroad.

633. Eva O. Fisher. Born 11 Jun 1880. Died ? .

She married Green Cave, 14 Oct 1897. Born ? . Died ? .

634. Leah Nora Fisher. Born 30 May 1884. Died 16 Jan 1964 in Taylor County, KY. Buried in Palestine Baptist Church Cemetery.

She married Mark T. Richeson, 29 Jan 1902. Born 2 Jul 1878. Died 10 Nov 1959.

635. Stella A. Fisher. Born 3 Jun 1887 in Taylor County, KY. Died 2 May 1978 in Taylor County, KY. Buried in Palestine Baptist Church Cemetery.

She married Omer H. Smith, 10 Dec 1908. Born 9 Mar 1885. Died 30 Aug 1973.

636. ? Fisher. Born 13 Feb 1895. Died 18 Mar 1895.

637. Virginia Fisher. Born 5 Mar 1895. Died ? .

638. T. T. Fisher. Born 19 Apr 1901. Died ? .

639. James Bruce Durbin. Born ? . Died ? .

640. Frances Durbin. Born ? . Died ? .

641. Ada Durbin. Born ? . Died ? .

642. Jesse Durbin. Born ? . Died ? .

643. Joseph Ambrose Durbin. Born ? . Died ? .

644. Mary Emma Durbin. Born ? . Died ? .

645. William Anthony Durbin. Born ? . Died ? .

646. Rhoda May Durbin. Born ? . Died ? .

647. Gibbon Durbin. Born ? . Died ? .

648. James William Witt. Born 9 May 1878. Died 12 Dec 1955.

649. Hester Jane Witt. Born 2 Jan 1880. Died Aug 1946.

650. George H. Witt. Born 27 Jan 1882. Died 7 Dec 1884.

651. Sarah Witt. Born 11 Mar 1884. Died 30 Nov 1884.

652. Carrie Witt. Born 3 Jan 1886. Died 10 Dec 1943.

653. John Q. Witt. Born 12 Apr 1888. Died 23 Jan 1944.

654. Owen O. Witt. Born 7 Sep 1890. Died ? .

655. Mayme Witt. Born 14 Sep 1893. Died 22 Aug 1918.

656. Anna Pearl Witt. Born 20 Aug 1895. Died ? .

657. Joe A. P. Witt. Born 24 Nov 1897. Died 27 Sep 1955.

658. Robert Vernon Witt. Born 16 Jan 1900. Died ? .

659. Lee Ella Witt. Born 22 Dec 1901. Died ? .

660. Maud Ella Witt. Born 22 Jan 1885 in Estill County, KY. Died 7 Feb 1888.

661. Bessie Lee Witt. Born 22 Feb 1887 in Estill County, KY. Died ? .

662. Gardner R. Witt. Born 30 Oct 1888 in Estill County, KY. Died 30 Aug 1917.

663. Earl Omer Witt. Born 4 Jun 1890 in Estill County, KY. Died 11 Sep 1957.

664. Emma Jane Witt. Born 25 Apr 1892 in Estill County, KY. Died 3 Aug 1943.

665. Hattie Lenora Witt. Born 17 Oct 1893 in Estill County, KY. Died ? .

666. Myrtle Witt. Born 29 Mar 1896 in Estill County, KY. Died ? .

667. Rhoda Susan Witt. Born 28 Feb 1898 in Estill County, KY. Died ? .

668. Ernest Yerkes Witt. Born 31 Jul 1900 in Estill County, KY. Died ? .

669. Leonard Raymond Witt. Born 30 May 1902 in Estill County, KY. Died 31 Oct 1903.

670. Lenna Clay Witt. Born 2 Jun 1904 in Estill County, KY. Died ? .

671. Eugene Kennon Witt. Born 30 Jul 1906 in Estill County, KY. Died ? .

672. Malie Emma Witt. Born ? . Died ? .

Information about the marriages and children is from Norton.

She first married Maurice Purvis. Born ? . Died ? . They had the following children:

869	i.	Hugh Purvis
870	ii.	Russell Purvis
871	iii.	Maurice Purvis
872	iv.	Addie Purvis

873	v.	Lula Purvis
874	vi.	Harry Purvis

She second married Robert Page. Born ? . Died ? . They had the following children:

875	i.	Claude Page
876	ii.	Hix Page
877	iii.	Mell Page
878	iv.	Bessie Page

673. Susan Bell Witt. Born ? . Died ? .

Information about the husband and children is from Norton.

She married T. Dan Hix. Born ? . Died ? . They had the following children:

879	i.	Janie Hix
880	ii.	Daniel Hix
881	iii.	Witt Hix
882	iv.	Susie Bell Hix

674. William Asa Witt. Born 20 Jan 1862 in Covington, VA. Died 20 Oct 1916.

All information is from Norton.

He married Lula Hubert, daughter of Benjamin Hubert, 7 Dec 1887 in Richmond, VA. Born 14 May 1865 in Lynchburg, VA. Died ? . They had the following children:

883	i.	William Hubert Witt

675. Joseph Henry Witt. Born ? . Died ? .

He married Gertie Rose. Born ? . Died ? (Norton).

676. Melville Lee Witt. Born ? . Died ? .

He married Maggie Darst. Born ? . Died ? (Norton).

677. Alonzo K. Witt. Born ? . Died ? .

678. John W. Witt. Born ? . Died ? .

679. Allie Witt. Born ? . Died ? .

She married ? Plunkett. Born ? . Died ? .

680. Silvie Witt. Born ? . Died ? .

She married ? Arnold. Born ? . Died ? .

681. Elizabeth Witt. Born ? . Died ? .

She married ? Ellis. Born ? . Died ? .

682. Woods Witt. Born ? . Died ? .

683. Mack Witt. Born ? . Died ? .

684. Sadie Witt. Born ? . Died ? .

685. Mattie Witt. Born ? . Died ? .

Information about the marriage and children is from Norton.

She married John H. Collins, in Staunton, VA. Born ? . Died ? .

They had the following children:

884	i.	Mary Elizabeth Collins
885	ii.	Sarah Frances Collins
886	iii.	Florence Dennet Collins
887	iv.	Willie Mattie Collins
888	v.	McWoods Collins
889	vi.	Sadie Collins
890	vii.	Lee G. Collins
891	viii.	Nancy Collins

686. Robert Witt. Born ? . Died ? .

687. Clinton Witt. Born ? . Died ? .

He married ? Patterson. Born ? . Died ? (Norton).

688. Charlie Witt. Born ? . Died ? .

Charlie never married (Norton).

689. Hattie Witt. Born ? . Died ? .

She married ? Loving. Born ? . Died ? (Norton).

690. Margaret Witt. Born ? . Died ? .

She married ? Loving. Born ? . Died ? (Norton).

691. Lucy Martin. Born ? . Died ? .

She married ? Wilkerson. Born ? . Died ? (Norton).

692. Dicie Martin. Born ? . Died ? .

She married Samuel Wright. Born ? . Died ? (Norton).

693. Mildred Martin. Born ? . Died ? .

She married ? Radcliff. Born ? . Died ? (Norton).

694. Nancy Martin. Born ? . Died ? .

She married ? Germany. Born ? . Died ? (Norton).

695. Constance Martin. Born ? . Died ? .

She married ? Bishop. Born ? . Died ? (Norton).

696. Isabella Hargis. Born 27 Feb 1858 in Allen County, KY. Died ? .

697. Margaret F. Hargis. Born 27 Dec 1859 in Allen County, KY. Died ? .

698. John D. Hargis. Born 5 Dec 1861 in Allen County, KY. Died ?

699. James L. Hargis. Born 1869 in Allen County, KY. Died ? .

700. Lula Hargis. Born Circa 1874 in Allen County, KY.

701. Lawretta Witt. Born 3 Oct 1866 in Allen County, KY. Died 22 Nov 1938 in Allen County, Ky. Buried in Maynard, New Bethel Church Cemetery.

She married Isaac H. (Dock) Owens. Born 18 Jul 1864. Died 9 Sep 1940 in Allen County, KY. Buried in Maynard, New Bethel Church Cemetery. They had the following children:

892	i.	Willie Owens
893	ii.	Dave Owens
894	iii.	Hugh Owens
895	iv.	Mary Owens
896	v.	Bess Owens
897	vi.	Pauline Owens

702. William H. Witt Jr. Born 1870 in Allen County, KY. Died ? .

He married Indiana ?. Born ? . Died ? .

703. George W. Witt. Born 7 Apr 1875 in Allen County, KY. Died 12 Dec 1951 in Allen County, KY. Buried in Maynard, New Bethel

Church Cemetery.

He married Eliza Maynard. Born 2 Feb 1879. Died 26 Mar 1969 in Allen County, KY. Buried in Maynard, New Bethel Church Cemetery. They had the following children:

898	i.	Louella Witt
899	ii.	Pearlie Witt
900	iii.	Jemmie Witt
901	iv.	John H. Witt
902	v.	Mary Etta Witt
903	vi.	George Everett Witt
904	vii.	India Mae Witt

704. John Witt. Born 28 Jun 1877 in Allen County, KY. Died 13 Jan 1941 in Allen County, KY. Buried in Maynard, New Bethel Church Cemetery.

John Married late in life. In the Census for 1910 he is listed as a boarder in the household of Robert Hood, and in the Census for 1920 he is listed as a member of the household of his sister and her husband Isaac Owens.

He married Hattie Garmon, 8 Jan 1931 in Allen County, KY. Born 1 Nov 1884. Died 2 Dec 1950 in Allen County, KY. Buried in Maynard, New Bethel Church Cemetery.

705. James F. Witt. Born 1880. Died ? .

706. James Letcher Witt. Born 24 Sep 1874 in Allen County, KY. Died 19 Aug 1943 in Allen County, KY. Buried in Maynard, New Bethel Church Cemetery.

He married Nancy E. Merritt. Born 1881. Died 1963 in Allen County, KY. Buried in Maynard, New Bethel Church Cemetery. They had the following children:

905	i.	Everett Witt

707. Henri Ella Witt. Born 9 Feb 1876 in Allen County, KY. Died 8 Oct 1949 in Allen County, KY. Buried in Mt. Gilead Church Cemetery.

She married John H. Cliburn. Born 6 Aug 1877. Died 24 Dec 1943 in Allen County, KY. Buried in Mt. Gilead Church Cemetery.

708. Elbridge Witt. Born 11 Aug 1879 in Allen County, KY. Died 3 Jan 1897 in Allen County, KY. Buried in Maynard, New Bethel Church Cemetery.

709. Charles Lon Witt. Born 24 Oct 1880 in Allen County, KY. Died 18 Jul 1944 in Allen County, KY. Buried in Maynard, New Bethel Church Cemetery.

He married Zula Hood, daughter of George Hood & Lucinda ?, 27 Dec 1904. Born 21 Aug 1886. Died 24 Nov 1978 in Allen County, KY. Buried in Maynard, New Bethel Church Cemetery. They had the following children:

906	i.	Robert Oldridge Witt
907	ii.	Margaret Helen Witt
908	iii.	Charles Witt

710. William Bertram Witt. Born 27 Jun 1883 in Allen County, KY. Died 7 Aug 1949 in Allen County, KY. Buried in Maynard, New Bethel Church Cemetery.

He married Birdella Dodson. Born 1893. Died 15 Oct 1961 in Scottsville, KY. Buried in Maynard, New Bethel Church Cemetery. They had the following children:

909	i.	Aubrey G. Witt

711. Herschell H. Witt. Born 6 Apr 1887 in Allen County, KY. Died 10 Jun 1950 in Allen County, KY. Buried in Maynard, New Bethel Church Cemetery.

He married Nellie B. Carver. Born 19 Apr 1900. Died 19 May 1986 in Indianapolis, IN. Buried in Maynard, New Bethel Church Cemetery. They had the following children:

910	i.	Sallie Mae Witt
911	ii.	Carrie Nell Witt

712. Lula Witt. Born 31 May 1889 in Allen County, KY. Died 5 May

1953 in Allen County, KY. Buried in Maynard, New Bethel Church Cemetery.

Lula never married.

713. Bettie Witt. Born 24 May 1893 in Allen County, KY. Died 18 Jul 1939 in Allen County, KY. Buried in Maynard, New Bethel Church Cemetery.

She married Ardor Meador. Born ? . Died ? . They had the following children:

 912 i. Ardie Meador

714. Capernia Witt. Born 1874. Died ? .

715. William T. Witt. Born 19 Oct 1875. Died 21 Dec 1914 in Allen County, KY. Buried in Clifton Church Cemetery.

William T. at some time moved from Barren to Allen County, where he married and where his children were born.

He married Minnie B. Hinton, daughter of Willis Hinton & Marandy Woodcock. Born 14 Sep 1879. Died 4 Nov 1959 in Allen County, KY. Buried in Clifton Church Cemetery. They had the following children:

 913 i. William L. Witt

 914 ii. William I. Witt

 915 iii. Zelma Witt

716. Nannie Witt. Born 1878. Died ? .

She married ? Witt. Born ? . Died ? . They had the following children:

 916 i. Maurice Witt

717. Robert E. Witt. Born 1879. Died 4 Nov 1923 in Barren County, KY. Buried in Barren County, Austin Cemetery (Leech and Beard 12).

718. Lucy Witt. Born 22 Aug 1884. Died 17 May 1910 in Barren County, KY. Buried in Barren County, Austin Cemetery (Leech and Beard 12).

719. Laura Witt. Born ? . Died 17 May 1910 in Barren County, KY. Buried in Austin Cemetery (Gorin, Deaths and Obituaries, 260).

720. Oscar Grayson Witt. Born 4 Apr 1872. Died 8 Sep 1928. Buried in Barren County, Pleasant Homes C. (Leech and Beard 405).

Oscar moved from Barren County to Allen; he is, however, buried in Barren County.

He first married Nancy McGinnis. Born Sep 1876. Died Before 1910. They had the following children:

917	i.	Roy Witt
918	ii.	Toy Witt
919	iii.	Lizzie Witt
920	iv.	Dave Witt
921	v.	Marvin Witt

He second married Lillie V. Pruitt, daughter of W. J. Pruitt & Janie Sikes. Born 23 Feb 1895. Died 6 Nov 1983 in Allen County, KY. Buried in Maynard, New Bethel Church Cemetery. They had the following children:

922	i.	Omer Witt
923	ii.	Harlin G. Witt
924	iii.	Aubrey Wilson Witt
925	iv.	Edna May Witt
926	v.	Mildred Witt
927	vi.	Magaline Witt
928	vii.	Evelyn Witt
929	viii.	Oscar Witt Jr.

721. James E. Witt. Born 1875. Died ? .

He married Lucy Sloan, daughter of Roan Sloan & Sallie Roberson, 29 Jan 1920 in Allen County, KY. Born ? . Died ? . They had the following children:

930	i.	Earl Witt
931	ii.	Opal D. Witt

722. Ora M. Witt. Born 1877. Died ? .

723. William F. Witt. Born 1879. Died ? .

724. Lon P. Witt. Born 22 Sep 1885. Died 17 May 1969. Buried in Glasgow Municipal C. (Leech and Beard 268).

He married Clara J. McIntire, 14 Feb 1917 in Allen County, KY. Born 2 Jun 1894. Died 28 May 1973 in Barren County, KY. Buried in Glasgow Municipal Cemetery (Leech and Beard 268). They had the following children:

    932   i.   Willis Freeman Witt

725. Cecil Witt. Born ? . Died 25 May 1982 in Scottsville, KY.

He married Alma H. McIntire, 14 Feb 1917 in Allen County, KY. Born ? . Died 8 Apr 1981 in Scottsville, KY. They had the following children:

    933   i.   Lucille Witt
    934   ii.   Cory Edward Witt
    935   iii.   J. C. Witt
    936   iv.   Willie B. Witt

726. Eleanor G. Witt. Born ? . Died ? .

727. Madie Witt. Born ? . Died ? .

She married ? O'Rork. Born ? . Died ? (Norton).

728. Daniel Witt. Born ? . Died ? .

729. Gordon Burgess Witt. Born ? . Died ? .

730. Maude Elizabeth Witt. Born ? . Died ? .

731. Mary Kathleen Witt. Born ? . Died ? .

732. Robert Hezikiah Witt. Born ? . Died ? .

733. Annie Kirk Witt. Born ? . Died ? .

734. Margaret Brand Witt. Born ? . Died ? .

735. William Randolph Witt. Born ? . Died ? .

736. Virginia Hierbemont Witt. Born ? . Died ? .

737. Dorcas Averett. Born ? . Died ? .

738. Elisha Averett. Born ? . Died ? .

739. Sarah Jane Averett. Born ? . Died ? .

740. Kizzie Ann Averett. Born ? . Died ? .

741. John Harvey Averett. Born ? . Died ? .

742. Elijah Averett. Born ? . Died ? .

743. George Averett. Born ? . Died ? .

744. Robert Wesley Averett. Born ? . Died ? .

745. James Lafayette Averett. Born ? . Died ? .

746. Lucy Lavinia Averett. Born ? . Died ? .

747. Jennette Eliza Averett. Born ? . Died ? .

748. Byron Averett. Born ? . Died ? .

749. David Averett. Born ? . Died ? .

750. Charley Flanary. Born ? . Died ? .

751. Susie Flanary. Born ? . Died ? .

She married Ballard Short. Born ? . Died ? (Lombardo).

752. Vilder Flanary. Born ? . Died ? .

753. Cornie Mae Flanary. Born 29 May 1888 in Virginia. Died ? .

She married Cammie Bush. Born ? . Died ? . They had the following children:

> 937   i.   Cammie Bush Jr.

754. William E. Flanary. Born 24 Sep 1890. Died ? .

755. Sally Flanary. Born 2 Apr 1896. Died ? .

She married Henry Short. Born ? . Died ? (Lombardo).

756. Corbin Flanary. Born 5 Sep 1905. Died ? .

757. Elsie Flanary. Born 30 Jul 1908. Died ? .

758. Andy Lee Witt. Born 26 Aug 1883. Died 13 Jun 1972.

Information about the marriage and children is from Laningham (337-338).

He married Bertie Fleenor, 7 Aug 1910. Born ? . Died ? . They had the following children:

> 938   i.   Floyd Winston Witt
>
> 939   ii.   Andy Lee Witt Jr.

940 iii. William C. Witt

941 iv. Mildred Fleenor Witt

759. Ida J. Witt. Born ? . Died ? .

She married ? Showalter. Born ? . Died ? (Laningham 337-338).

760. Charles R. Witt. Born ? . Died ? .

761. Edily Florence Witt. Born ? . Died ? .

She married Winfield S. Rose. Born ? . Died ? (Laningham 337-338).

762. Leonard L. Witt. Born ? . Died ? .

He married Bezmonia Litton, daughter of Andrew J. Litton & Joanna Cecil. Born ? . Died ? (Laningham 337-338).

763. Billie Allen Allen. Born ? . Died ? .

764. Hiram Leroy Brockman Jr. Born 24 May 1921 in Greer, SC.

765. David Dean Brockman. Born 4 Aug 1922 in Greer, SC.

766. Betty Lou Brockman. Born 11 Jan 1925. Died 19 Jan 1928.

767. Cassie Huff. Born 3 Feb 1908 in Harlan County, KY. Died 26 Feb 1980 in Harlan County, KY.

Information about the marriage and children is from Lombardo.

She married Chester Witt, son of John Wesley Witt & Mary Doss, 4 May 1929 in Harlan County, KY. Born 7 Nov 1909 in Holmes Mill, KY. Died 14 Dec 1962 in Harlan County, KY.

They had the following children:

942 i. Georgia Witt

943 ii. Billy O'Neal Witt

944 iii. Edna Cleo Witt

768. Ferrell Huff. Born ? .

769. Ballard Kelly Jr.

770. Flossie Holmes. Born ? .

771. Glenda Holmes. Born 1934 in Harlan County, KY.

772. Edgar Holmes. Born ? .

773. Wilmer Holmes. Born ? .

774. Delonia Holmes. Born 8 May 1913 in Harlan County, KY. Died Mar 1988 in Holmes Mill, KY.

Information about the wife and children is from Lombardo.

She married Lawrence Witt, son of John Wesley Witt & Mary Doss. Born 7 Jun 1912 in Harlan County, KY. They had the following children:

945	i.	Dovie Witt
946	ii.	Darshall Witt
947	iii.	Wavo Witt
948	iv.	Arcelia Witt
949	v.	Rodney Witt
950	vi.	Sonja Witt

775. Celia Holmes. Born 6 Mar 1918 in Harlan County, KY.

Lombardo indicates that Celia is a stepchild.

She married Earl Edmond Witt, son of John Wesley Witt & Mary Doss. Born 22 Jun 1922 in Harlan County, KY. Died 13 Dec 1987 in Harlan County, KY. They had the following children:

951	i.	Yolanda Witt
952	ii.	Veronica Witt
953	iii.	Juliet Witt
954	iv.	Earl Edmond Witt Jr.
955	v.	Haran Edmond Witt
956	vi.	Lillie Lavonne Witt

776. Lana Holmes. Born ? .

777. Kermit Holmes. Born ? .

778. Comrad Holmes. Born ? .

779. Bertha M. Witt. Born 22 Apr 1907 in Harlan, KY. Died 2 Jun 1923 in Laurel County, KY.

780. Dillard Witt. Born 10 Jul 1909 in Harlan, KY. Died 21 Feb 1984 in Lexington, KY. Buried 24 Feb 1984 in Owsley Cemetery, London, KY.

Information about the marriage and children is from Lombardo.

He married Sallie Bowling, daughter of Jessie Bowling & Alabama Whitis, 22 Dec 1926 in Laurel County, KY. Born 1 Sep 1910 in Clay County, KY. Died 30 Jun 1985 in London, KY. Buried 3 Jul 1985 in Owsley Cemetery, London, KY. They had the following children:

957	i.	Julia Marie Witt
958	ii.	Zelma Lee Witt
959	iii.	Andrew Jessie Witt
960	iv.	Homer Birchel Witt
961	v.	Willard Eugene Witt
962	vi.	Unnamed Witt
963	vii.	Chester Roy Witt
964	viii.	Dillard Douglas Witt
965	ix.	Shirley Diane Witt
966	x.	Troy Cy Witt

781. Rushia Witt. Born 12 Jul 1912 in Harlan, KY.

782. Grant Witt. Born 2 Apr 1915 in Harlan, KY. Died 29 Aug 1929 in Laurel County, KY.

783. Fred Witt. Born 3 Mar 1917 in Harlan, KY. Died 22 Mar 1917 in Harlan, KY.

784. Newton Witt. Born 28 May 1919 in Harlan, KY.

Information about the marriage and children is from Lombardo.

He married Ola Mae Wynn, 13 Jan 1940 in Laurel County, KY. Born ? . They had the following children:

967	i.	Cleo Elizabeth Witt
968	ii.	Carol Ann Witt

785. Earl Witt. Born 4 Feb 1922 in Harlan, KY. Died 17 Mar 1922 in Harlan, KY.

786. Ruby Witt. Born 6 May 1923 in Laurel County, KY.

787. Verlia Opal Witt. Born 10 Jan 1926 in Laurel County, KY.

788. John Carter Witt. Born 7 Jul 1928 in Laurel County, KY.

789. Harlen Ray Witt. Born 2 Aug 1932 in Laurel County, KY. Died 13 Dec 1935 in Laurel County, KY.

790. Howard Witt. Born 7 Feb 1908. Died 22 May 1977 in Harlan County, KY.

Information about the marriage and children is from Lombardo.

He married Rossie Mae Robbins, daughter of Mack Robbins & Eunice Rutherford, 1 Jan 1935 in Harlan County, KY. Born ? . They had the following children:

969	i.	Wanda Ketrenia Witt
970	ii.	Vealah Cosette Witt
971	iii.	Archie Ercil Witt
972	iv.	Duskie Delores Witt
973	v.	Regina Witt

791. Chester Witt. Born 7 Nov 1909 in Holmes Mill, KY. Died 14 Dec 1962 in Harlan County, KY.

Information about the wife and children is from Lombardo.

He married Cassie Huff, daughter of Bill Huff & Mary Short, 4 May 1929 in Harlan County, KY. Born 3 Feb 1908 in Harlan County, KY. Died 26 Feb 1980 in Harlan County, KY. They had the following children:

942	i.	Georgia Witt
943	ii.	Billy O'Neal Witt
944	iii.	Edna Cleo Witt

792. Lawrence Witt. Born 7 Jun 1912 in Harlan County, KY.

Information about the wife and children is from Lombardo.

He married Delonia Holmes, daughter of Wiley Holmes & Lily Victoria Short. Born 8 May 1913 in Harlan County, KY. Died Mar 1988 in Holmes Mill, KY. They had the following children:

945	i.	Dovie Witt
946	ii.	Darshall Witt

947	iii.	Wavo Witt
948	iv.	Arcelia Witt
949	v.	Rodney Witt
950	vi.	Sonja Witt

793. Otis Witt. Born 23 Nov 1914.

Information about the wife and children is from Lombardo.

He married Hestel Robbins, daughter of Palmer Robbins & Mary Holmes, 8 Apr 1933 in Harlan County, KY. Born ? . They had the following children:

974	i.	J. C. Witt
975	ii.	Inez Wavolene Witt
976	iii.	Betty Rosetta Witt
977	iv.	Donnie Ray Witt

794. Clercia Witt. Born 13 Mar 1917 in Harlan County, KY.

Information about the husband and children is from Lombardo.

She married Bradley Kelly, son of Filmore Kelly & Dora ?, 10 Aug 1935. Born ? . They had the following children:

978	i.	Clayton Odell Kelly
979	ii.	Mildred Sue Kelly
980	iii.	Teresa Mary Kelly
981	iv.	Tina Renaee Kelly
982	v.	David Bradley Kelly

795. Vilder Witt. Born 17 Jan 1920.

Information about the wife and children is from Lombardo.

He married Beatrice Short. Born ? . They had the following children:

983	i.	Ruth Witt
984	ii.	Armaina Witt
985	iii.	Barnie Merle Witt
986	iv.	Jenny Witt
987	v.	Ola Mae Witt

988   vi.   Shirley Ilene Witt

796. Earl Edmond Witt. Born 22 Jun 1922 in Harlan County, KY. Died 13 Dec 1987 in Harlan County, KY.

Information about the husband and children is from Lombardo.

He married Celia Holmes, daughter of Wiley Holmes & Lily Victoria Short. Born 6 Mar 1918 in Harlan County, KY. Lombardo indicates that Celia is a stepchild. They had the following children:

951   i.   Yolanda Witt

952   ii.   Veronica Witt

953   iii.   Juliet Witt

954   iv.   Earl Edmond Witt Jr.

955   v.   Haran Edmond Witt

956   vi.   Lillie Lavonne Witt

797. Beulah Witt. Born 14 Nov 1924.

Information about the marriage and children is from Lombardo.

She married William Carl Huff, son of B. Huff & Maggie Whisman, 6 Aug 1940 in Harlan County, KY. Born ? . They had the following children:

989   i.   Ronald J. Huff

990   ii.   Linda Huff

991   iii.   Cheryl Darlene Huff

798. Ada Witt. Born 12 Nov 1926.

Information about the marriage and children is from Lombardo.

She married Cammie Bush Jr., son of Cammie Bush & Cornie Mae Flanary, 23 Feb 1948 in Harlan County, KY. Born ? . They had the following children:

992   i.   Donna Gail Bush

993   ii.   Lennis Randy Bush

994   iii.   Vicki Lynn Bush

799. Geneva Charity Witt. Born 17 May 1929 in Harlan County, KY.

Information about the marriage and children is from Lombardo.

She married Earl Howard, son of Lloyd Howard & Florence Jackson, 19 Jul 1947 in Harlan County, KY. Born ? . They had the following children:

995	i.	Ricky Darrel Howard
996	ii.	Connie Ann Howard
997	iii.	Earl Howard Jr.
998	iv.	John Terry Howard

800. Orcia Witt. Born 23 Nov 1914 in Harlan County, KY.

Information about the marriage and children is from Lombardo.

He married Wilma Moore, daughter of Ernest Moore & Pearlie Hoskins, 28 May 1955 in Sneedsville, TN. Born ? . They had the following children:

999	i.	Sharon Rena Witt
1000	ii.	Michael Eric Witt

801. Oakie Witt. Born ? .

She married Ernest Bledsoe, 1946 in Harlan County, KY. Born ? (Lombardo).

802. Alpha Witt. Born ? .

803. Sue Witt. Born ? .

Information about the husband and children is from Lombardo.

She married Arthur Parker, son of John Parker & Easter Halcomb. Born ? . They had the following children:

1001	i.	Larry Parker
1002	ii.	Linda Parker
1003	iii.	Vickie Parker

804. Hazel King. Born ? .

805. Nora Witt. Born ? .

806. Alton Witt. Born ? .

807. Louise Witt. Born ? .

She married ? Jordan. Born ? (Lombardo).

808. Sandra Witt. Born ? .

She married ? Combs. Born ? (Lombardo).

809. Gwen Witt. Born ? .

810. John Elbert Frank. Born ? . Died ? .

811. William Anderson Frank. Born ? . Died ? .

812. Ruth Witt. Born 24 Sep 1914 in Liberty, KY.

She married Ezra Ashley. Born 1 Apr 1911. Died May 1990 in Pulaski County, KY. They had the following children:

1004	i.	Ezra Carroll Ashley
1005	ii.	Joaline Ashley
1006	iii.	Harold Glen Ashley
1007	iv.	Robert Newell Ashley
1008	v.	Rutheda Dean Ashley
1009	vi.	Gerald Witt Ashley

813. Ruby Witt. Born 11 Apr 1913 in Casey County, KY. Died 3 Feb 1976 in Cincinnati, OH. Buried in Spring Grove Cemetery, Cincinnati, OH.

She first married Ralph Cecil Hansford. Born Circa 1908. Died ? . They had the following children:

1010	i.	Suzanne Hansford
1011	ii.	Ralph Cecil Hansford Jr.

She second married John Jack Francis. Born ? .

814. Samuel Joseph Witt Jr. Born 22 Sep 1911 in Casey County, KY. Died 14 Dec 1977 in Cincinnati, OH.

Samuel Joseph, Jr., taught school in Liberty, KY. He married Jessie Dean King, 27 Nov 1932 in Casey County, KY. Born 24 Feb 1914 in Casey County, KY. Died ? . They had the following children:

1012	i.	Joseph King Witt
1013	ii.	Darrell Willard Witt
1014	iii.	Samuel Alfred Witt

1015   iv.   Carolyn Lou Witt

815. Arthur Witt. Born 12 Nov 1890 in Casey County, KY. Died 31 Aug 1960 in Casey County, KY.

He married Zipora (Zipoah) Grider, 6 Jan 1912 in Casey County, KY. Born 1886. Died 1947. Buried in Glenwood Cemetery. They had the following children:

1016   i.   Bessie Witt

816. Otha Witt. Born 28 Sep 1892 in Casey County, KY. Died 2 Oct 1892 in Casey County, KY. Buried in Fair Cemetery.

817. Leslie Green Witt. Born 11 Sep 1894 in Liberty, KY. Died 19 Jul 1966 in Franklin, IN.

He married Laura Goode. Born 2 Aug 1898 in Liberty, KY. Died 15 Jan 1951 in Franklin, IN. They had the following children:

1017   i.   Clifton Witt

1018   ii.   Max Witt

1019   iii.   Audra Witt

1020   iv.   Helen Ailene Witt

1021   v.   Sally (Frances) Witt

1022   vi.   Pauline J. Witt

1023   vii.   Norman Lee Witt

1024   viii.   Betty Lois Witt

818. Virgil A. Witt. Born 31 Mar 1896 in Casey County, KY. Died 15 Jan 1965 in Evansville, IN.

He married Lillie Grider. Born ? . Died ? . They had the following children:

1025   i.   Bertha Witt

1026   ii.   James E. Witt

819. Curtis Witt. Born 13 Jul 1898 in Casey County, KY. Died 18 Apr 1957 in Cairo, IL.

He married Mattie Leona Bullard, 29 Oct 1921 in Charleston, MO. Born 23 Mar 1903 in Mississippi County, MO. Died 14 Apr 1988 in Sikeston, MO. Buried in Oak Grove Cemetery, Charleston, MO. They had the following children:

1027	i.	Dorothy Virginia Witt
1028	ii.	Glen Curtis Witt
1029	iii.	Leta Oneda Witt
1030	iv.	Lonnie Dale Witt
1031	v.	Herbert Louis Witt
1032	vi.	Wilbur Lee Witt
1033	vii.	Orvel Wayne Witt

820. Herman Witt. Born 29 Nov 1899 in Casey County, KY.

He married Rose Foster, 29 Aug 1922 in Liberty, KY. Born 20 Jul 1900 in Liberty, KY. Died 24 Jul 1986 in Cincinnati, OH. They had the following children:

| 1034 | i. | Lily May Witt |

821. Clyde Witt. Born 1 Jan 1902 in Casey County, KY. Died 12 Nov 1989 in Franklin, IN.

He married Helen Gaunce, 1922. Born Circa 1907. Died ? in Morgantown, IN. They had the following children:

1035	i.	Clyde Witt II
1036	ii.	Loran D. Witt
1037	iii.	Denny Witt
1038	iv.	James Robert Witt
1039	v.	Benny Witt
1040	vi.	Samuel W. Witt
1041	vii.	Elizabeth Jane Witt
1042	viii.	Nancy Witt
1043	ix.	David Witt

822. James Witt. Born 31 Dec 1903 in Casey County, KY. Died 28 Sep 1967 in California.

He married Alice ?. Born ? . Died ? .

823. Edgar Witt. Born 18 Nov 1890 in Casey Co, KY. Died 24 Dec

1956. Buried in Glenwood Cemetery.

Information about the children is from Gendex.

He first married Mattie Bell, 23 Dec 1912. Born Circa 1896. Died ? .

He second married Lola Etta Sharp. Born 1892 in Casey Co, KY. Died 1934. Buried in Glenwood Cemetery, Liberty, KY. They had the following children:

1044	i.	Edgar Witt Jr.
1045	ii.	Evelyn Witt
1046	iii.	Ruby Mae Witt
1047	iv.	Nancy Frances Witt
1048	v.	Lula Mabel Witt
1049	vi.	Charles Sherman Witt II
1050	vii.	Clarence Lee Witt
1051	viii.	Betty Ruth Witt

824. Luther Witt. Born 13 Apr 1892 in Liberty, KY. Died 8 Apr 1973 in Liberty, KY.

He married Maude Eller Allen, 17 Dec 1911 in Liberty, KY. Born 2 Mar 1896 in Casey Co, KY. Died 2 Mar 1994 in Clinton, IL. They had the following children:

1052	i.	Paul Maward Witt
1053	ii.	Edith Lanere Witt
1054	iii.	James S. Witt
1055	iv.	Edgar Howard Witt
1056	v.	George Wallace Witt
1057	vi.	Lela M. (Marie?) Witt
1058	vii.	Mildred Opal Witt
1059	viii.	Roberta Witt
1060	ix.	Mary E. Witt
1061	x.	Luther Witt Jr.

825. Oscar Witt. Born 5 Mar 1894 in Casey County, KY. Died 26

May 1991. Buried in Ninevah, IN.

He first married Ella Magaline Thompson, 14 Jan 1912 in Casey County, KY. Born 3 Dec 1895 in Casey County, KY. Died 31 Jul 1945 in Knoxville, TN. They had the following children:

1062	i.	Arla Louise Witt
1063	ii.	Arlis Edward Witt
1064	iii.	Bessie Kathryn Witt
1065	iv.	Orville Clifton Witt
1066	v.	Boy Witt
1067	vi.	Edward Witt
1068	vii.	Elizabeth (Bessie) Witt

He second married Lillie Mills, 1945 in Johnson County, IN. Born 8 Sep 1906 in Pinkstaff, IL. Died 1995 in Johnson County, IN.

826. Della Witt. Born 18 Nov 1896 in Casey County, KY. Died 1973. Buried in Glenwood Cenetery.

She married James Edgar Price. Born Circa 1892. Died ? . They had the following children:

1069	i.	Preston Price
1070	ii.	Alma Fay Price

827. Sally E. Witt. Born 27 Apr 1899 in Casey County, KY. Died 15 May 1990 in Salem, IN.

She married Samuel Estill Wells. Born 21 Jul 1897 in Corbin, KY (?). Died 21 Feb 1966 in Salem, IN. They had the following children:

1071	i.	Cecil Ambrose Wells
1072	ii.	Hazel Margaret Wells
1073	iii.	Mildred Marie Wells
1074	iv.	Richard Eugene Wells
1075	v.	Samuel Estill Wells Jr.

828. Alnier Witt. Born Circa 1893. Died 12 Apr 1904.

Alnier died of convulsions.

829. Ada Witt. Born 1895. Died ? . Buried in Fair Cemetery.

830. Albert Witt. Born Circa 1897. Died ? .

831. Claude Witt. Born Circa 1899. Died ? .

832. Ethel Witt. Born Circa 1901. Died ? .

833. Almer Witt. Born 1903. Died ? . Buried in Fair Cemetery.

834. Myrtle Witt. Born Circa 1905. Died ? .

835. Stanley Pete Witt. Born 1 Jun 1907. Died ? .

He married ? Rogers. Born ? . Died ? . They had the following children:

    1076   i.   Dillard Witt

    1077   ii.   Bernice Witt

836. Adell Witt. Born Circa 1909. Died ? .

837. Mildred Witt. Born Circa 1911. Died ? .

838. Lorene Witt. Born Circa 1913. Died ? .

839. Charles Witt. Born 1916. Died 1944 in Liberty, KY. Buried in Salem U.M. Church Cemetery.

Charles was killed in WW II.

840. Earl Witt. Born 23 Jan 1904 in Casey County, KY. Died 30 Nov 1966 in Casey county, KY.

He married Mary Taylor, Circa 1926 in Casey County, KY. Born ? in Liberty, KY. Died 29 May 1982 in Liberty, KY. Buried in Antioch Christian Church Cemetery. They had the following children:

    1078   i.   Cecil Eugene Witt

    1079   ii.   Virginia Lee Witt

    1080   iii.   Betty Sue Witt

841. Audrey Witt. Born 12 May 1907. Died 1963.

She married Clell Sanders. Born ? . They were divorced.

842. Beulah Witt. Born Circa 1921.

She married Carl Davis. Born Circa 1921.

843. . Born ? .

844. Jack Evans. Born ? . Died ? .

845. Georgia Fay Witt. Born Circa 1906. Died ? .

846. Lucy Fay Witt. Born 1916. Died 1922.

847. Lillian Witt. Born Circa 1916. Died ? .

She married Dewy Hansford. Born Circa 1911. Died ? . They had the following children:

    1081   i.   Wanda Hansford

848. Forest Witt. Born Circa 1928.

849. Elizabeth Witt. Born Circa 1930.

850. Kathlene Witt. Born Circa 1932.

851. Lillie May Witt. Born Circa 1934.

852. Unnamed. Born ? . Died ? .

853. Carl Ellis. Born ? . Died ? .

854. Margie Ellis. Born ? . Died ? .

855. Virgie (Virginia) Ellis. Born ? . Died ? .

856. Adopted. Born ? . Died ? .

857. Helen Patricia Crockett. Born Circa 1916 in Greenwood, IN.

She married William E. McShurley, Circa 1936. Born Circa 1911.

858. Charles Marvin Hill. Born 20 Jan 1907 in Taylor County, KY. Died ? .

He married Montye Mae Minor, 26 Dec 1936 in Jefferson County, KY. Born 18 Oct 1914 in Taylor County, KY. Died ? .

859. Lucille Hill. Born ? .

She married Lefrey Colvin. Born ? .

860. Ruby Hill. Born ? .

She married Herbert Hall. Born ? .

861. Carl Hill. Born ? .

He married Gertrude Keltner. Born ? .

862. Edmonston Hill. Born ? .

He married Dorthy Van Dyke. Born ? .

863. Clementine Hill. Born ? .

She married Jack Sapp. Born ? .

864. Muriel Hill. Born ? .

She married Vernon Auston. Born ? .

865. Dorotha Hill. Born ? .

She married Willard Winfrey. Born ? .

866. Jack Hill. Born ? .

He married Reva Simmons. Born ? .

867. Catherine Herron. Born ? . Died ? .

868. Chester Herron. Born ? . Died ? .

869. Hugh Purvis. Born ? . Died ? .

870. Russell Purvis. Born ? . Died ? .

871. Maurice Purvis. Born ? . Died ? .

872. Addie Purvis. Born ? . Died ? .

873. Lula Purvis. Born ? . Died ? .

874. Harry Purvis. Born ? . Died ? .

875. Claude Page. Born ? . Died ? .

876. Hix Page. Born ? . Died ? .

877. Mell Page. Born ? . Died ? .

878. Bessie Page. Born ? . Died ? .

879. Janie Hix. Born ? . Died ? .

880. Daniel Hix. Born ? . Died ? .

881. Witt Hix. Born ? . Died ? .

882. Susie Bell Hix. Born ? . Died ? .

She married ? Winston. Born ? . Died ? (Norton).

883. William Hubert Witt. Born 8 Oct 1888. Died ? .

Information about the marriage and children is from Norton.

He married Lucy Drummond Brooke, 31 Mar 1910 in Norfolk, VA. Born ? . Died ? . They had the following children:

1082	i.	Tucker Brooke Witt
1083	ii.	William Asa Witt
1084	iii.	Robert Brooke Witt

884. Mary Elizabeth Collins. Born ? . Died ? .

She married Robert Ramsey. Born ? . Died ? (Norton).

885. Sarah Frances Collins. Born ? . Died ? .

She married Frank Snyder. Born ? . Died ? (Norton).

886. Florence Dennet Collins. Born ? . Died ? .

She married Floyd Lotts. Born ? . Died ? (Norton).

887. Willie Mattie Collins. Born ? . Died ? .

She married Frank Lotts. Born ? . Died ? (Norton).

888. McWoods Collins. Born ? . Died ? .

889. Sadie Collins. Born ? . Died ? .

She married Ernest Taylor. Born ? . Died ? (Norton).

890. Lee G. Collins. Born ? . Died ? .

He married H. B. Forsythe. Born ? . Died ? (Norton).

891. Nancy Collins. Born ? . Died ? .

892. Willie Owens. Born ? . Died ? .

Since I have only the name for Willie and no other information, I am not certain whether she is female or male.

893. Dave Owens. Born ? . Died ? .

894. Hugh Owens. Born ? . Died ? .

895. Mary Owens. Born ? . Died ? .

896. Bess Owens. Born ? . Died ? .

897. Pauline Owens. Born ? . Died ? .

898. Louella Witt. Born 2 Mar 1899. Died ? .

She married Virgil Whitney, son of Charlie Whitney & Lucy Jackson, 22 Jul 1923 in Allen County, KY. Born 27 Feb 1893. Died 2 Aug 1968. Buried in Maynard, New Bethel Church Cemetery. They had the following children:

    1085   i.   Nellie Whitney

    1086 ii.   James Whitney

899. Pearlie Witt. Born 1903. Died ? .

She married ? Harston. Born ? . Died ? . They had the following children:

1087   i.   William E. Harston

900. Jemmie Witt. Born 7 Apr 1905. Died 27 Feb 1988 in Allen County, KY. Buried in Maynard, New Bethel Church Cemetery.

She married Hillius Cornwell, son of Ed Cornwell & Maggie Bridges, 5 Sep 1929 in Allen County, KY. Born 24 Apr 1904. Died 28 Oct 1986 in Allen County, KY. Buried in Maynard, New Bethel Church Cemetery.

901. John H. Witt. Born 8 Aug 1908. Died 29 Aug 1992 in Allen County, KY. Buried in Maynard, New Bethel Church Cemetery.

He first married ?. They had the following children:

1088   i.   John Larry Witt

He second married Lula Francis Counts, daughter of Tommy Farley & Lillie Stinson, 10 Oct 1964 in Allen County, KY. Born ? . Died ? .

902. Mary Etta Witt. Born 29 Apr 1911. Died 14 Mar 1996 in Allen County, KY. Buried in Maynard, New Bethel Church Cemetery.

She first married Marvin Witt, son of Oscar Grayson Witt & Nancy McGinnis. Born 20 Nov 1907. Died 25 Aug 1931 in Allen County, KY. Buried in Maynard, New Bethel Church Cemetery.

She second married Sim Tinsley, 19 Oct 1946. Born 3 Mar 1911. Died 19 May 1992 in Allen County, KY. Buried in Maynard, New Bethel Church Cemetery.

903. George Everett Witt. Born 12 Dec 1913. Died 3 Oct 1978 in Allen County, KY. Buried in Scottsville, Crescent Hill Cemetery.

He married Ruth Ritchey, 4 Nov 1938. Born 21 Aug 1922. They had the following children:

1089   i.   Everette Wayne Witt

1090   ii.   Margaret Ann Witt

1091   iii.   Lareca Witt

904. India Mae Witt. Born 15 Nov 1916.

She married Robert Tinsley, son of R. C. Tinsley & Millie Pitcock, 26 Dec 1938 in Allen County, KY. Born 1 Mar 1914. Died 9 Apr 1977 in Allen County, KY. Buried in Maynard, New Bethel Church Cemetery.

905. Everett Witt. Born ? . Died ? .

Everette and his wife lived in Warren County; they had no children. He was an educator and served for a time as superintendent of the Warren County schools.

He married ?.

906. Robert Oldridge Witt. Born 15 Oct 1906 in Allen County, KY. Died 3 May 1936 in Warren County, KY. Buried in Maynard, New Bethel Church Cemetery.

Oldridge and Elizabeth died tragically of gunshot wounds; their deaths were ruled a murder and a suicide, but several questions remain unanswered. They had no children.

He married Elizabeth Bishop. Born 27 Nov 1911. Died 3 May 1936 in Warren County, KY. Buried in Maynard, New Bethel Church Cemetery.

907. Margaret Helen Witt. Born 3 Sep 1915 in Allen County, KY. Died ? in Allen County, KY.

She married Barton Warren Downing Jr., son of Barton Warren Downing & Bessie Austin, 27 Aug 1932 in Allen County, KY. Born ? . Died ? . They had the following children:

    1092 i.   Margaret Neal Downing

908. Charles Witt. Born 6 Oct 1927 in Allen County, KY. Died 31 Aug 1954 in Warren County, KY. Buried in Maynard, New Bethel Church Cemetery.

Charles died in an automobile crash. He married Clytie Mann. Born ? . They had the following children:

    1093 i.   Sherry Neal Witt

1094   ii.   Charles Robert Witt

909. Aubrey G. Witt. Born Jul 1912 in Allen County, KY. Died Oct 1986 in Scottsville, KY. Buried in Maynard, New Bethel Church Cemetery.

He married Nina Loyce Cook, daughter of Orbin C. Cook & Nellie M. Harris, 1933 in Glasgow, KY. Born 17 Aug 1915. They had the following children:

1095   i.   Robert W. Witt

910. Sallie Mae Witt. Born 2 Jul 1921 in Allen County, KY. Died 15 May 1993 in Indianapolis, IN. Buried in Maynard, New Bethel Church Cemetery.

Delbert and Sallie Mae lived in Indianapolis; they had no children.

She married Delbert Howard. Born 24 May 1918.

911. Carrie Nell Witt. Born 26 May 1932 in Allen County, KY.

Glenn and Carrie Nell live in Indianapolis; I have no information about their children.

She married Glenn Howard, son of Jack Howard & Bell Emberton, 25 Dec 1950 in Allen County, KY. Born ? .

912. Ardie Meador. Born ? . Died ? .

Since I have no information other than the name, I am not certain whether Ardie is female or male.

913. William L. Witt. Born 20 Nov 1909 in Allen County, KY. Died 5 Aug 1928 in Allen County, KY. Buried in Clifton Church Cemetery.

914. William I. Witt. Born 16 Nov 1911 in Allen County, KY. Died 16 Nov 1911 in Allen County, KY.

An unnamed Witt is listed in the birth records as the infant of William and Minnie Bell Hinton born on 16 Nov 1911 in Allen County; the death records list the death of William I. Witt on 16 Nov 1911 in Allen County. I am not certain, though, that William I. is the son of

William and Minnie B. Witt.

915. Zelma Witt. Born 18 Sep 1913 in Allen County, KY.

She married W. Lermond Whitney, 13 Jan 1943. Born 8 Apr 1907. Died 18 Jan 1983. Buried in Allen County, KY, New Hope Cemetery. They had the following children:

    1096   i.   Willie Louise Whitney

916. Maurice Witt. Born 30 Jul 1913 in Barren County, KY.

She married ? McIntyre. Born ? . Died ? . They had the following children:

    1097   i.   Freeman McIntyre

    1098   ii.   Frank McIntyre

    1099   iii.   Caroline McIntyre

917. Roy Witt. Born 6 Nov 1894. Died 31 Aug 1921 in Allen County, KY. Buried in Maynard, Bethel Church Cemetery.

He married Walsey Lena Ledford, daughter of Sam Ledford & Mary Ann Adcock, 6 Jun 1918 in Allen County, KY. Born ? . Died ? . They had the following children:

    1100   i.   Viola Witt

    1101   ii.   Roy Witt Jr.

918. Toy Witt. Born 16 Dec 1896. Died 18 Jun 1919. Buried in Maynard, New Bethel Church Cemetery.

She married Lee D. Farley. Born 1872. Died 1943. Buried in Maynard, New Bethel Church Cemetery. They had the following children:

    1102   i.   Mildred Farley

919. Lizzie Witt. Born May 1899. Died 18 Feb 1916. Buried in Maynard, New Bethel Church Cemetery.

920. Dave Witt. Born 1905. Died 25 Jan 1929.

In the funeral record Gardner lists Marion Witt as the only survivor of Dave (192). I do not know what the relationship was, whether wife, daughter, or son.

921. Marvin Witt. Born 20 Nov 1907. Died 25 Aug 1931 in Allen County, KY. Buried in Maynard, New Bethel Church Cemetery.

He married Mary Etta Witt, daughter of George W. Witt & Eliza Maynard. Born 29 Apr 1911. Died 14 Mar 1996 in Allen County, KY. Buried in Maynard, New Bethel Church Cemetery.

922. Omer Witt. Born 28 Feb 1911. Died 12 Feb 1927 in Allen County, KY. Buried in Maynard, New Bethel Church Cemetery.

923. Harlin G. Witt. Born 26 Dec 1912.

He first married Clarene Davis, daughter of Ed Davis & Tilly Spivey, 24 Nov 1935 in Allen County, KY. Born ? . They had the following children:

    1103   i.   Helen Dean Witt

He second married Zelma Blankenship, daughter of Will Bullington & Mary Hogue, 19 Dec 1963 in Allen County, KY. Born ? .

924. Aubrey Wilson Witt. Born 5 Jan 1916. Died 4 Jul 1979 in Allen County, KY. Buried in Maynard, New Bethel Church Cemetery.

He married Dorothy Buchanan. Born 30 Jul 1920. Died 7 Jan 1982. Buried in Maynard, New Bethel Church Cemetery. They had the following children:

    1104   i.   Charles W. Witt
    1105   ii.   Dorothy A. Witt
    1106   iii.   Dana J. Witt
    1107   iv.   Phyllis C. Witt
    1108   v.   Janie L. Witt
    1109   vi.   Jackie R. Witt
    1110   vii.   Dwight H. Witt
    1111   viii.   Jeffrey Scott Witt
    1112   ix.   Lisa Dianne Witt

925. Edna May Witt. Born 14 Jul 1918.

She married ? Witt. Born ? . Died ? . They had the following children:

1113   i.   Geneva L. Witt

926. Mildred Witt. Born 22 Mar 1921.

She married Ewell Graves, son of Burton Graves & Claudie Hyde, 9 Mar 1940 in Allen County, KY. Born ? . They had the following children:

1114   i.   Brenda Graves

1115   ii.   Martha L. Graves

927. Magaline Witt. Born 4 Aug 1923.

She married Sam Hatten Linville, son of K. Linville & Ivy Bridges, 16 Dec 1941 in Allen County, KY. Born ? . Died ? . They had the following children:

1116   i.   Sam Linville Jr.

1117   ii.   Cara Linville

928. Evelyn Witt. Born 4 Aug 1923.

She married Jess Hunt, 30 May 1941. Born 1917. Died 1947. They had the following children:

1118   i.   Orville Hunt

1119   ii.   Jesse Hunt

929. Oscar Witt Jr. Born 14 Sep 1927.

He married Novice Jewell Petty, daughter of William Jewell Petty & Mary Susan Owens, 3 May 1947 in Allen County, KY. Born ? . They had the following children:

1120   i.   Teresa L. Witt

930. Earl Witt. Born 14 Jun 1921.

931. Opal D. Witt. Born 31 May 1925.

932. Willis Freeman Witt. Born 21 Sep 1917. Died 6 Oct 1918 in Barren County, KY. Buried in Pleasant Homes Cemetery (Leech and Beard 405).

933. Lucille Witt. Born 10 Oct 1917. Died 10 Aug 1918. Buried in Pleasant Homes Cemetery (Leech and Beard 405).

934. Cory Edward Witt. Born ? . Died 7 Dec 1935. Buried in

Pleasant Homes Cemetery (Leech and Beard 405).

935. J. C. Witt. Born ? .

936. Willie B. Witt. Born ? .

937. Cammie Bush Jr. Born ? .

Information about the marriage and children is from Lombardo.

He married Ada Witt, daughter of John Wesley Witt & Mary Doss, 23 Feb 1948 in Harlan County, KY. Born 12 Nov 1926. They had the following children:

992	i.	Donna Gail Bush
993	ii.	Lennis Randy Bush
994	iii.	Vicki Lynn Bush

938. Floyd Winston Witt. Born ? . Died ? .

939. Andy Lee Witt Jr. Born ? . Died ? .

940. William C. Witt. Born ? . Died ? .

941. Mildred Fleenor Witt. Born ? . Died ? .

942. Georgia Witt. Born ? in Harlan County, KY. Died ? in Florida.

Information about the husband and children is from Laningham and Lombardo.

She married Earl Poff. Born ? . They had the following children:

1121	i.	Michael Poff
1122	ii.	David Poff
1123	iii.	Mark Poff

943. Billy O'Neal Witt. Born ? in Harlan County, KY.

Information about the husband and children is from Lombardo.

He married Nola Jeanette Kelly, daughter of Henry Kelly & Gertrude Cox. Born ? . They had the following children:

1124	i.	Carolyn Lou Witt
1125	ii.	Billy O'Neal Witt Jr.

944. Edna Cleo Witt. Born ? .

945. Dovie Witt. Born 30 Dec 1933 in Harlan County, KY.

Information about the husbands and children is from Lombardo.

She first married Ray Hamblin. Born ? . They had the following children:

    1126   i.   Monica Hamblin

    1127   ii.   Derek Hamblin

She second married Walter Smith, 1996. Born ? .

946. Darshall Witt. Born 12 May 1937 in Harlan County, KY.

947. Wavo Witt. Born 25 Aug 1942 in Harlan County, KY.

Information about the wife and children is from Lombardo.

He married Wanda Bray, daughter of George Bray & Love Wynn. Born ? . They had the following children:

    1128   i.   Keith Witt

    1129   ii.   Jeremy Witt

948. Arcelia Witt. Born 14 Mar 1947 in Harlan County, KY.

Information about the husband and children is from Lombardo.

She married David Bowman, son of Joe Bowman & Sallie Howard. Born ? . They had the following children:

    1130   i.   Dustin Bowman

    1131   ii.   Brandon Bowman

949. Rodney Witt. Born 5 Aug 1949 in Harlan County, KY.

Information about the wife and children is from Lombardo.

He married Sharon Short, daughter of General Short & Dezzie Hazel. Born ? . They had the following children:

    1132   i.   Connie Witt

    1133   ii.   Tracy Witt

950. Sonja Witt. Born 12 Aug 1957 in Harlan, KY.

Information about the marriage and children is from Lombardo.

She married Colen Terry Kelly, 3 Jan 1977. Born ? . They had the following children:

    1134   i.   Stacie Lynn Kelly

1135   ii.   Nevada Terrian Kelly

951. Yolanda Witt. Born 22 Mar 1942 in Harlan County, KY.

Information about the marriage and children is from Lombardo.

She married Billy Gerald Kelly, son of Henry Kelly & Gertrude Cox, 7 Jun 1968 in East Stone Gap, VA. Born ? . They had the following children:

1136   i.   Elizabeth Victoria Kelly

1137   ii.   Carmen Stacie Kelly

952. Veronica Witt. Born 25 Feb 1944 in Harlan County, KY.

Information about the husband and children is from Lombardo.

She married Jack Johnson. Born ? . They had the following children:

1138   i.   Kimberly A. Johnson

1139   ii.   Stacie Lynn Johnson

953. Juliet Witt. Born 26 Sep 1945 in Harlan County, KY.

Information about the marriage and children is from Lombardo.

She married William Delmar Clark, 21 Aug 1966. Born ? . They had the following children:

1140   i.   William Craig Clark

1141   ii.   Verlanda Kenona Clark

1142   iii.   Judel Keturah Clark

954. Earl Edmond Witt Jr. Born 12 Jan 1949 in Harlan County, KY. Died 12 Jan 1949 in Harlan County, KY.

955. Haran Edmond Witt. Born 22 May 1951 in Harlan County, KY.

Information about the wife and children is from Lombardo.

He married Coleen Kelly, daughter of Clarence Kelly & Juanita ?. Born ? . They had the following children:

1143   i.   Ronald Witt

1144   ii.   Steven Witt

1145   iii.   Nicholas Witt

956. Lillie Lavonne Witt. Born 7 Apr 1954 in Harlan County, KY. Information about the husband and children is from Lombardo. She married Glen Allen Roberts, son of Glen Roberts & Jean ?. Born ? . They had the following children:

    1146 i.   Johnny Ray Roberts

    1147 ii.   Edmond Allen Roberts

    1148 iii.   Celia Jean Roberts

    1149 iv.   Glen Earl Roberts

    1150 v.   Jasmine Moon Roberts

957. Julia Marie Witt. Born 16 Nov 1927 in Laurel County, KY. Died 3 Dec 1927.

958. Zelma Lee Witt. Born 8 Oct 1928 in Laurel County, KY. Information about the marriage and child is from Lombardo. She married Raymond Clarence Edwards, 15 May 1954 in Jellico, TN. Born ? . They had the following children:

    1151 i.   Carol Elizabeth Edwards

959. Andrew Jessie Witt. Born 26 Sep 1929 in Laurel County, KY. Died 20 Jun 1994 in London, KY. Buried 23 Jun 1994 in Owsley Cemetery, London, KY.

960. Homer Birchel Witt. Born 2 Dec 1931 in Laurel County, KY.

961. Willard Eugene Witt. Born 25 Feb 1935 in Laurel County, KY.

Information about the marriage and children is from Lombardo. He married Jeannie Babbette Nelson, 21 Jul 1956 in Los Angeles, CA. Born ? . They had the following children:

    1152 i.   Douglas Eugene Witt

    1153 ii.   Dean Evan Witt

    1154 iii.   Troy Kevin Witt

    1155 iv.   Barry Alan Witt

962. Unnamed Witt. Born 1937 in Laurel County, KY. Died 1937.

963. Chester Roy Witt. Born 4 Aug 1938 in Laurel County, KY.

Information about the marriage is from Lombardo.

He married June Partin, 5 May 1984 in Los Angeles, CA. Born ?

964. Dillard Douglas Witt. Born 6 Mar 1942 in London, KY.

Information about the marriage and children is from Lombardo.

He married Frances Marie Kelly, 16 Apr 1966 in Marquette, MI.

Born 26 Sep 1943. They had the following children:

    1156   i.   Douglas Scott Witt

    1157   ii.   Steven Paul Witt

965. Shirley Diane Witt. Born 18 Sep 1947 in Laurel County, KY.

Information about the marriage and children is from Lombardo.

She married Berton Dugger, 2 Jul 1964 in London, KY. Born 3 Mar 1945. They had the following children:

    1158   i.   Denise Dugger

    1159   ii.   Sarah Dugger

966. Troy Cy Witt. Born 16 Feb 1951 in London, KY.

Information about the marriage and children is from Lombardo.

He married Brenda Kay Creech, 20 Feb 1969 in London, KY.

Born 2 Feb 1953. They had the following children:

    1160   i.   Amy Lynn Witt

    1161   ii.   Rebecca Kay Witt

967. Cleo Elizabeth Witt. Born 3 Aug 1941 in Laurel County, KY.

968. Carol Ann Witt. Born 8 Jan 1956 in Detroit, MI.

969. Wanda Ketrenia Witt. Born 4 Oct 1935 in Holmes Mill, KY.

Information about the marriages and children is from Lombardo.

She first married Jimmy Farley, 25 Dec 1954 in Harlan County, KY. Born ? . They had the following children:

    1162   i.   Deborah Ann Farley

    1163   ii.   Pamela Jean Farley

She second married Leonard Saverio Lombardo, 4 Jul 1975 in Berea, KY. Born ? .

970. Vealah Cosette Witt. Born 1 Jan 1939.

Information about the husbands and children is from Lombardo.

She first married Carl Short, son of Andrew Short & Mary Kelly. Born ? . They had the following children:

    1164   i.   Vernon Short

    1165   ii.   Joy Gayle Short

She second married Daivd Thomas. Born ? .

971. Archie Ercil Witt. Born 5 Apr 1943 in Harlan County, KY.

Information about the marriage and children is from Lombardo.

He married Barbara Short, daughter of Roy Short & Loetta Huff, 27 Dec 1963 in Harlan County, KY. Born ? . They had the following children:

    1166   i.   Mike Witt

    1167   ii.   Lisa Witt

972. Duskie Delores Witt. Born 29 Jun 1947 in Harlan County, KY. Died 26 Dec 1992 in Harlan County, KY.

Information about the marriage and children is from Lombardo.

She married Winston Caudill, son of Finley Caudill & Varlie ?, 29 Aug 1964 in Harlan County, KY. Born ? . They had the following children:

    1168   i.   Bruce Winston Caudill

    1169   ii.   Jerry Caudill

    1170   iii.   Jerry Howard Caudill

    1171   iv.   Crystal Dianne Caudill

973. Regina Witt. Born 9 Sep 1962 in Harlan County, KY.

Information about the marriages and children is from Lombardo.

She first married Russell Messer, 17 Nov 1977 in Harlan County, KY. Born ? . They had the following children:

    1172   i.   Christina Messer

She second married Jeff Mayo, 16 Aug 1986. Born ? . They had the following children:

1173 i. Scott Mayo

974. J. C. Witt. Born 30 Aug 1934 in Holmes Mill, KY. Died 3 May 1987 in Evarts, KY.

Information about the marriage and children is from Lombardo.

He married Geneva Schuler, 28 Nov 1959 in Harlan County, KY. Born ? . They had the following children:

1174 i. Jeffrey Craig Witt

1175 ii. Jennifer Carol Witt

1176 iii. Janice Crystal Witt

975. Inez Wavolene Witt. Born 24 Mar 1936 in Harlan County, KY.

Information about the marriage and children is from Lombardo.

She married Kenneth Poff, 15 May 1954. Born ? . They had the following children:

1177 i. Tim Poff

1178 ii. Connie Poff

976. Betty Rosetta Witt. Born 20 Aug 1943.

Information about the marriage and children is from Lombardo.

She married Jimmy Darrell Frazier, 26 Nov 1964 in Harlan County, KY. Born ? . They had the following children:

1179 i. Ronnie Darrell Frazier

1180 ii. Brian Keith Frazier

977. Donnie Ray Witt. Born 20 Sep 1946 in Harlan County, KY.

Information about the wife and children is from Lombardo.

He married Teresa Sears. Born ? . They had the following children:

1181 i. John Christopher Witt

1182 ii. Tonya Renee Witt

1183 iii. Sonya Kay Witt

1184 iv. Angela Kay Witt

1185 v. Timothy Wayne Witt

978. Clayton Odell Kelly. Born 21 Feb 1938 in Harlan County, KY.

He married Erika Hergurg. Born ? (Lombardo).

979. Mildred Sue Kelly. Born 25 Jan 1941 in Harlan County, KY.

980. Teresa Mary Kelly. Born 27 Feb 1943 in Harlan County, KY.

981. Tina Renaee Kelly. Born 14 Jul 1945.

She married Garnie Clark. Born ? (Lombardo).

982. David Bradley Kelly. Born 17 Mar 1949 in Harlan County, KY.

983. Ruth Witt. Born ? .

Information about the husband and children is from Lombardo.

She married Whetsel Thomas. Born ? . They had the following children:

1186	i.	Delilah Thomas
1187	ii.	Beatrice Thomas
1188	iii.	Murl Thomas
1189	iv.	Toy Thomas
1190	v.	Marty Thomas
1191	vi.	Anna Margaret Thomas
1192	vii.	Marsha Thomas

984. Armaina Witt. Born ? .

She married Clayton Huff. Born ? (Lombardo).

985. Barnie Merle Witt. Born ? .

Information about the marriage and children is from Lombardo.

He married Jo Ann Blair, daughter of Dexter Blair & Pebbles Barton, 21 Dec 1963 in Harlan County, KY. Born ? . They had the following children:

1193	i.	Steven Dexter Witt
1194	ii.	Brandon Paul Witt

986. Jenny Witt. Born ? .

987. Ola Mae Witt. Born ? .

988. Shirley Ilene Witt. Born ? .

989. Ronald J. Huff. Born 5 May 1941 in Harlan County, KY.

990. Linda Huff. Born 27 Jul 1948 in Harlan County, KY.

She married Tom Smith, 9 Jul 1988 in Mareno, Ohio. Born ? . (Lombardo).

991. Cheryl Darlene Huff. Born 5 Jul 1958 in Mount Gilead, Ohio.

992. Donna Gail Bush. Born 26 Oct 1949 in Wise County, VA.

993. Lennis Randy Bush. Born 27 Apr 1952 in Wise County, VA.

994. Vicki Lynn Bush. Born 5 Oct 1958 in Wise County, VA.

995. Ricky Darrel Howard. Born 17 Mar 1948 in Lee County, VA.

996. Connie Ann Howard. Born 4 Feb 1950.

997. Earl Howard Jr. Born 7 Nov 1954 in Mt. Gilead, Ohio.

998. John Terry Howard. Born 26 Dec 1956 in Mt. Gilead, Ohio.

999. Sharon Rena Witt. Born 31 Mar 1956 in Mt. Gilead, Ohio.

Information about the marriage and children is from Lombardo.

She married Larry Jay Hildebrand, son of Leslie Hildebrand & Ester Houseburger, 22 Nov 1988 in Marengo, Ohio. Born ? . They had the following children:

> 1195   i.   John Leslie Hildebrand
>
> 1196   ii.   James Jay Hildebrand
>
> 1197   iii.   Sarah Jean Hildebrand

1000. Michael Eric Witt. Born 2 Oct 1960 in Mt. Gilead, Ohio.

Information about the marriage and children is from Lombardo.

He married Jean McCurdy, daughter of Russell McCurdy & Mary Houck, 20 Jun 1980 in Marengo, Ohio. Born ? . They had the following children:

> 1198   i.   Michael Benjamin Witt
>
> 1199   ii.   Nicholas Eric Witt

1001. Larry Parker. Born ? .

1002. Linda Parker. Born ? .

1003. Vickie Parker. Born ? .

1004. Ezra Carroll Ashley. Born Circa 1934 in Casey County, KY.
He married Rose Ellen Brewer, Circa 1952. Born Circa 1934 in
Indiana.

1005. Joaline Ashley. Born Circa 1935.
She first married Wendell Sloan. Born ? .
She second married Robert Collier, Aug 1965. Born Circa 1940.

1006. Harold Glen Ashley. Born 2 Jun 1937.
He first married Barbara Jo Lee, Circa 1957 in Pulaski County,
KY. Born ? .
He second married Jackie ?, Circa 1970. Born ? .

1007. Robert Newell Ashley. Born 4 Nov 1940.
He married Velma Sue Belcher, Circa 1959 in Eubank, KY.
Born Circa 1940.

1008. Rutheda Dean Ashley. Born 21 Sep 1945.

1009. Gerald Witt Ashley. Born 25 Nov 1947 in Waynesburg, KY.
He married Rebecca Faye Ray, 3 Jun 1972 in Halls Gap, KY.
Born 23 Jun 1952 in Bedford, IN.

1010. Suzanne Hansford. Born 21 May 1946 in Cincinnati, OH.
She married Charles Wesley Poppe, 25 May 1968 in Cincinnatti.
Born 21 Nov 1946 in Lebanon, OH.

1011. Ralph Cecil Hansford Jr. Born 31 Dec 1931 in Casey
County, KY. Died 15 May 1996.
He married Dorothy Huddelston, Circa 1949 in Cincinnati, OH.
Born 7 Apr 1933 in Cincinnati, OH.

1012. Joseph King Witt. Born 27 Aug 1935. Died 27 Dec 1986.
He married Myrtle Hyden, 6 Jun 1957. Born ? . Died ? . They
had the following children:

1200	i.	Linda Gail Witt
1201	ii.	Roger Clark Witt
1202	iii.	Ronald Ross Witt

1013. Darrell Willard Witt. Born 14 Apr 1938.

He married Sharon Powell, 5 Oct 1968 in Covington, KY. Born ? . They had the following children:

1203	i.	Linda Marie Witt
1204	ii.	Charles Adrian Witt
1205	iii.	Robert Douglas Witt
1206	iv.	Michelle Renee Witt

1014. Samuel Alfred Witt. Born 4 Nov 1941 in Casey County, KY. Died 8 Dec 1972 in Williamstown, KY.

He first married Barbara Everheardt. Born ? .

He second married Nedra Karen Carpenter, Circa 1971. Born ? . They had the following children:

1207	i.	Nathan Samuel Witt

1015. Carolyn Lou Witt. Born 6 Mar 1949 in Danville, KY.

She first married Donald Joseph Greene, 4 Sep 1971. Born ? .

She second married Raymond Terrance Clark, 14 Apr 1979 in Cincinnatti. Born 20 Sep 1951 in Cincinnatti. They had the following children:

1208	i.	Megan Rae Clark

1016. Bessie Witt. Born Circa 1914.

She married Perry Iredle Gallimore. Born Circa 1913 in Ohio. Died ? . They had the following children:

1209	i.	Deems Taylor Gallimore

1017. Clifton Witt. Born 2 Jul 1920 in Charleston, MO. Died 17 Aug 1986 in Franklin, IN.

He married Marjorie Marie Barger, 17 May 1940 in Johnson County, IN. Born 16 Mar 1922 in Johnson County, IN. They had the following children:

1210	i.	William Gordon Witt
1211	ii.	Ronald Clifton Witt
1212	iii.	Kenneth Wayne Witt

1018. Max Witt. Born 6 Oct 1929 in Liberty, KY. Died 4 Feb 1935 in Franklin, IN.

1019. Audra Witt. Born 28 Feb 1924 in Charleston, MO. Died 3 Jan 1943 in Franklin, IN.

1020. Helen Ailene Witt. Born Circa 1925 in Charleston, MO.

She first married Robert Guinnup, 1949. Born ? . They had the following children:

1213	i.	Stephen Guinnup

She second married Elmer Clyde Quick, 21 May 1969 in Greenwood, IN. Born 7 Nov 1917 in Johnson County, IN. Died 7 Jan 1995 in Johnson County, IN.

1021. Sally (Frances) Witt. Born 1927 in Charleston, MO.

She first married ? Miller. Born ? .

She second married Richard Fergason, 1945 in Johnson County, IN. Born 17 Jan 1922. Died 14 Apr 1967 in Franklin, IN. They had the following children:

1214	i.	Richard D. Fergason

1022. Pauline J. Witt. Born 13 Nov 1932. Died 4 Apr 1950 in Franklin, IN.

1023. Norman Lee Witt. Born 19 Jul 1933.

He married Mary Ellen Mann, 31 Aug 1958 in Johnson County, IN. Born 26 Oct 1937. They had the following children:

1215	i.	Laura Lee Witt
1216	ii.	Kevin Matthew Witt
1217	iii.	Barry Jay Witt
1218	iv.	Douglas Brian Witt
1219	v.	Craig Allen Witt
1220	vi.	Kristine Kay Witt

1024. Betty Lois Witt. Born 10 Mar 1940 in Johnson County, IN.

She married John Nathan Morris, 28 Oct 1961 in Franklin, IN. Born 11 Nov 1927. They had the following children:

    1221   i.   Jonathan Nathan Morris Jr.

1025. Bertha Witt. Born Circa 1923.

She married ? Goebel. Born ? . They had the following children:

    1222   i.   Gerald Goebel

1026. James E. Witt. Born Circa 1925.

1027. Dorothy Virginia Witt. Born 4 Apr 1925 in Franklin, IN.

She married Donald Keith King, 26 May 1944 in Franklin, IN. Born ? .

1028. Glen Curtis Witt. Born 4 Dec 1926 in Elmwood Place, OH.

He married Marion Jean Angelly, 19 Sep 1952. Born ? . They had the following children:

    1223   i.   Linda Renee Witt

    1224   ii.   Karen Marie Witt

1029. Leta Oneda Witt. Born 28 Dec 1928 in Cincinnati, OH. Died 20 Jun 1992 in Sikeston, MO.

She married Stanley Dean Jollift. Born ? .

1030. Lonnie Dale Witt. Born 28 Sep 1930 in Franklin, IN.

He married Betty Jo Hawkins, 30 Apr 1955 in Franklin, IN. Born ? .

1031. Herbert Louis Witt. Born 8 Jan 1937 in Mississippi County, MO. Died 4 Jun 1938 in Charleston, MO.

1032. Wilbur Lee Witt. Born 28 Oct 1940 in Charleston, MO.

He married Gwendolynn Sue Fields Ellis, 9 Mar 1963 in Charleston, MO. Born ? . They had the following children:

    1225   i.   David Witt

1033. Orvel Wayne Witt. Born 9 Jun 1944 in Charleston, MO.

He married Carolyn Ann Mayo, 14 Nov 1964. Born 7 Jan 1946 in Cairo, IL. They had the following children:

1226	i.	Randall Wayne Witt
1227	ii.	Julie Ann Witt
1228	iii.	Donna Kay Witt

1034. Lily May Witt. Born 9 Nov 1921 in Casey County, KY.
She married Darrel Dallas Yeazel, 4 Jul 1941 in Covington, KY.
Born 6 Mar 1921 in Reading, OH. They had the following children:

1229	i.	Tahanna Ann Yeazel
1230	ii.	Darrel Duane Yeazel II

1035. Clyde Witt II. Born Circa 1923.
He married Beulah ?. Born ? .

1036. Loran D. Witt. Born Circa 1925.

1037. Denny Witt. Born Circa 1927.

1038. James Robert Witt. Born 9 Oct 1928.
He married Rosemary Clark. Born ? . They had the following children:

1231	i.	James Robert Witt II

1039. Benny Witt. Born 1930.

1040. Samuel W. Witt. Born Circa 1932.
He married Mary D. Edwards, 1947. Born ? .

1041. Elizabeth Jane Witt. Born Circa 1934.
She married Lyle Wayne Stillabower, 1948. Born ? . They had the following children:

1232	i.	Jill Stillabower
1233	ii.	Don Stillabower

1042. Nancy Witt. Born Circa 1936.

1043. David Witt. Born 1943.

1044. Edgar Witt Jr. Born ? .

1045. Evelyn Witt. Born ? .

1046. Ruby Mae Witt. Born ? .

1047. Nancy Frances Witt. Born ? .

1048. Lula Mabel Witt. Born ? .

1049. Charles Sherman Witt II. Born Circa 1929.

1050. Clarence Lee Witt. Born Circa 1931.

1051. Betty Ruth Witt. Born Circa 1934.

1052. Paul Maward Witt. Born 12 Feb 1913 in Casey County, KY.
He married Mary Ann Taylor, 4 Nov 1933 in Casey County,
KY. Born 12 Mar 1913. Died 7 Sep 1981 in Clinton, IL. They had the
following children:

      1234   i.   Roger Witt

      1235   ii.   Joyce Witt

      1236   iii.   Infant

1053. Edith Lanere Witt. Born 30 Dec 1915 in Casey County, KY.
She married Jim Taylor, 15 Jun 1934 in Somerset, KY. Born 3
Apr 1913 in Casey County, KY. They had the following children:

      1237   i.   Jenette Taylor (Twin)

      1238   ii.   Julia Taylor (Twin)

      1239   iii.   Pam Taylor

1054. James S. Witt. Born 23 Jun 1917 in Casey County, KY. Died
31 Jul 1918 in Casey County, KY. Buried in Allens Cemetery, Casey
County, KY.

1055. Edgar Howard Witt. Born 2 Jan 1919 in Casey County, KY.
He married Elva Manilla Bowmer, 23 Jan 1943 in Jamestown,
KY. Born 19 Oct 1919 in Casey County, KY. They had the following
children:

      1240   i.   JoAnne Witt

      1241   ii.   Patsy Dale Patty Witt

1056. George Wallace Witt. Born 9 Apr 1921 in Liberty, KY.
He first married Irene Thompson, 5 Dec 1946 in Lawrenceburg,
KY. Born 9 Oct 1922 in Casey County, KY. Died 24 Feb 1977 in Boyle
County, KY. They were divorced. They had the following children:

      1242   i.   Donna Jean Witt

      1243   ii.   Waunda Lou Witt

1244   iii.   Larry Ray Witt

He second married Lena Ione Walker. Born 16 Nov 1917 in Muhlenburg County, KY.

He third married Lola Watson, 10 Nov 1986 in Shelbyville, KY. Born ? .

1057. Lela M. (Marie?) Witt. Born 6 Apr 1923 in Casey County, KY. Died 1 May 1923 in Casey County, KY.

Lela died at six weeks old. Maude, her mother, was too sick with pneumonia to care for her so Mary Bell, her grandmother, was babysitting. She gave Lela cow's milk which killed her. Mary Bell was beginning to lose her full faculties.

1058. Mildred Opal Witt. Born 25 Jun 1924 in Casey County, KY.

She married Richard Lane (Dick) Helm, 9 Oct 1943 in Danville, KY. Born 4 Jan 1915 in Marion County, KY. Died 18 Mar 1989 in Louisville, KY. Buried in Greenwood Cemetery, Liberty, KY. They had the following children:

1245   i.   Richard Wayne Helm
1246   ii.   Jerry Helm
1247   iii.   Sandra Kay Helm

1059. Roberta Witt. Born 8 Jun 1927 in Casey County, KY.

She married Lucien Atwood, 15 Jul 1944. Born 2 Feb 1925 in Casey County, KY. Died 5 Nov 1991. They had the following children:

1248   i.   Betty Jean Atwood
1249   ii.   Linda Sue Atwood

1060. Mary E. Witt. Born 29 Oct 1930 in Casey Co, KY. Died 29 Oct 1930 in Casey Co, KY.

1061. Luther Witt Jr. Born 20 Apr 1934.

He married Peggy Vest. Born ? . They had the following children:

1250   i.   Charlene Witt
1251   ii.   Francine Witt

1252	iii.	Annette Witt
1253	iv.	Denise Witt
1254	v.	Teresa Witt

1062. Arla Louise Witt. Born 4 Nov 1915.

She first married Jim Jeffries. Born ? . They had the following children:

1255	i.	James Nelson Jeffries
1256	ii.	Glenda Gail Jeffries
1257	iii.	Girl Jeffries

She second married ? Holscher. Born ? .

1063. Arlis Edward Witt. Born 13 Dec 1917 in Casey County, KY.

He first married Wavey Gertrude Lynn, 12 Dec 1935 in Jamestown, KY. Born 30 Dec 1919. Died 28 Mar 1977 in Casey County, KY. They had the following children:

1258	i.	Carlis Dean Witt
1259	ii.	Mona Carol Witt
1260	iii.	Dorotha Sue Witt

He second married Ann Collins, in Mississippi. Born 1 May 1924. Died 1 Sep 1995.

1064. Bessie Kathryn Witt. Born 7 Jul 1919.

She first married Jesse Lynn. Born ? in Casey County, KY. Died Circa 1975 in Indiana. They had the following children:

| 1261 | i. | Bobby Sherill Lynn |
| 1262 | ii. | Wanda Lou Lynn |

She second married James Rullo, 23 Sep 1946 in Middletown, OH. Born 23 May 1922 in Pennsylvania. They had the following children:

| 1263 | i. | Dana Marc (Danny) Rullo |

1065. Orville Clifton Witt. Born 9 May 1921. Died 1966 in Tafalgers, IN.

He married Elizabeth Richards. Born Circa 1926 in Bowling

Green, KY. They had the following children:

      1264 i.   Patty Witt

      1265 ii.   Linda Witt

1066. Boy Witt. Born Circa 1923.

1067. Edward Witt. Born Circa 1925.

      He first married Wavy Lyn. Born ? .

      He second married Ann ?. Born ? .

1068. Elizabeth (Bessie) Witt. Born Circa 1927.

      She married Jim (?) Ruello. Born ? .

1069. Preston Price. Born Circa 1913. Died 1957.

      He married Gerty Bell. Born Circa 1916.

1070. Alma Fay Price. Born 3 Nov 1915 in Casey County, KY.

      She married Ralph Wilkerson. Born 5 Oct 1912 in Casey
County, KY. Died 17 Oct 1985 in Casey County, KY.

1071. Cecil Ambrose Wells. Born 15 Dec 1916 in Casey County,
KY. Died 17 Dec 1977 in Casey County, KY.

      He married Esther (May) Thompson, 5 Oct 1935 in Casey
County, KY. Born 8 Dec 1916 in Casey County, KY.

1072. Hazel Margaret Wells. Born 23 Sep 1920 in Kentucky. Died
1 May 1992 in Salem, IN.

      She married Louie Roney, in Salem, IN. Born 9 Sep 1917 in
Iowa.

1073. Mildred Marie Wells. Born 8 Apr 1923 in East Bernstadt,
KY.

      She married Herbert Owen Moores, 11 Jan 1941 in Cincinnati,
OH. Born 2 Jan 1918 in Dayton, OH.

1074. Richard Eugene Wells. Born 24 Aug 1930 in Indiana.

      He married Pat White. Born ? .

1075. Samuel Estill Wells Jr. Born 27 Dec 1938 in Washington
County, IN.

      He first married Carol Purlee. Born Circa 1945.

He second married Gle-Etta ?. Born Circa 1946.

He third married Cathleen Cecelia Hoerst. Born Circa 1939.

1076. Dillard Witt. Born Circa 1931 in Ohio (?).

1077. Bernice Witt. Born Circa 1932 in Ohio (?).

1078. Cecil Eugene Witt. Born 4 Jun 1927 in Casey County, KY.

He married Betty Jean Estes, 24 Feb 1951 in Yosemite Nazarene, KY. Born 10 Apr 1931 in Casey County, KY. They had the following children:

> 1266　i.　　Belinda Gail Witt
>
> 1267　ii.　　Jill Witt
>
> 1268　iii.　　Gina Lynn Witt

1079. Virginia Lee Witt. Born 4 Sep 1930.

She married Harold Ray Wilson, 29 Dec 1951 in Lexington, KY. Born 15 Nov 1931. They had the following children:

> 1269　i.　　Steven Ray Wilson

1080. Betty Sue Witt. Born 5 Jul 1946 in Danville, KY.

She married Alvie Atwood, 25 Feb 1967 in Liberty, KY. Born 13 Sep 1942. They had the following children:

> 1270　i.　　Wendy Paige Atwood
>
> 1271　ii.　　Robyn Renee Atwood

1081. Wanda Hansford. Born Circa 1947.

1082. Tucker Brooke Witt. Born 6 Sep 1911. Died ? .

1083. William Asa Witt. Born 18 Jun 1913. Died ? .

1084. Robert Brooke Witt. Born 17 Apr 1915. Died ? .

1085. Nellie Whitney. Born 22 Aug 1924.

1086. James Whitney. Born 31 Mar 1927.

1087. William E. Harston. Born 8 Oct 1928.

1088. John Larry Witt. Born ? .

1089. Everette Wayne Witt. Born 10 Jan 1942.

He married Bonnie Lou King, daughter of William King & Edith Spencer, 9 Jun 1962 in Allen County, KY. Born ? . They had the following children:

    1272 i.   Kevin Dewayne Witt

1090. Margaret Ann Witt. Born 29 May 1947.

    She married William Allen. Born ? . They had the following children:

    1273 i.   Tonya Allen

1091. Lareca Witt. Born 18 Sep 1955.

    She first married Billy Miller. Born ? . They had the following children:

    1274 i.   Billy J. Miller

    She second married Randy Byrn. Born ? . They had the following children:

    1275 i.   Alicia Byrn

1092. Margaret Neal Downing. Born 1938 in Fountain Run, KY.

    She married Jack Brown Jr., son of Jack Brown & Marie ?, 27 Aug 1960 in Scottsville, KY. Born 1933 in Celina, TN. They had the following children:

    1276 i.   Jacqueline N. Brown

    1277 ii.   Charles F. Brown

    1278 iii.   Hugh B. Brown

1093. Sherry Neal Witt. Born 27 Sep 1950.

1094. Charles Robert Witt. Born 3 Mar 1954.

1095. Robert W. Witt. Born 26 Mar 1937 in Allen County, KY.

1096. Willie Louise Whitney. Born 23 Oct 1943.

1097. Freeman McIntyre. Born 12 Jun 1940 in Allen County, KY.

1098. Frank McIntyre. Born 8 Aug 1943 in Barren County, KY.

1099. Caroline McIntyre. Born 9 Mar 1949 in Barren County, KY.

1100. Viola Witt. Born 1919.

1101. Roy Witt Jr. Born 1 Oct 1921.

1102. Mildred Farley. Born 21 Sep 1916 in Allen County, KY.

1103. Helen Dean Witt. Born 22 Apr 1937.

She married J. D. Willoughby, son of Charles Odell Willoughby & Elsie Margaret Horne, 18 Sep 1959 in Allen County, KY. Born ? . They had the following children:

    1279   i.   Deborah Willoughby

    1280 ii.   Laurie Willoughby

1104. Charles W. Witt. Born 29 Jan 1938.

1105. Dorothy A. Witt. Born 5 Aug 1940.

1106. Dana J. Witt. Born 6 Jul 1947.

1107. Phyllis C. Witt. Born 7 Nov 1948.

1108. Janie L. Witt. Born 29 Jan 1950.

1109. Jackie R. Witt. Born 23 Sep 1951.

1110. Dwight H. Witt. Born 5 Nov 1952.

1111. Jeffrey Scott Witt. Born 25 Sep 1959.

He married Caroline Sue Poland, daughter of Reed Poland & Ruth Hayes, 26 Dec 1981 in Allen County, KY. Born ? . They had the following children:

    1281   i.   Joshua S. Witt

1112. Lisa Dianne Witt. Born ? .

She married Danny Melvin Carter, son of Robert M. Carter & Ina Farley, 6 Nov 1982 in Allen County, KY. Born ? . They had the following children:

    1282   i.   Chad Carter

    1283 ii.   Holly Carter

1113. Geneva L. Witt. Born 21 Jan 1937.

1114. Brenda Graves. Born 14 Jan 1942.

1115. Martha L. Graves. Born 4 Nov 1945.

1116. Sam Linville Jr. Born 31 Aug 1942.

1117. Cara Linville. Born 24 Mar 1950.

1118. Orville Hunt. Born 3 Mar 1942. Died 10 Dec 1945.

1119. Jesse Hunt. Born 28 Sep 1942.

The date of Jesse's birth must be incorrect, but that is the date in the birth records.

1120. Teresa L. Witt. Born 17 Oct 1954.

She married Porter Barton. Born ? . They had the following children:

    1284 i.   James M. Barton

1121. Michael Poff. Born ? .

1122. David Poff. Born ? .

1123. Mark Poff. Born ? .

1124. Carolyn Lou Witt. Born 4 Mar 1952.

1125. Billy O'Neal Witt Jr. Born 16 Jan 1954.

1126. Monica Hamblin. Born 20 Sep 1973.

1127. Derek Hamblin. Born 18 Sep 1983.

1128. Keith Witt. Born 26 Jul 1970 in Harlan County, KY.

Information about the wife and child is from Lombardo.

He married Ida Howard. Born ? . They had the following children:

    1285 i.   Amber Witt

1129. Jeremy Witt. Born 14 Oct 1978.

1130. Dustin Bowman. Born 15 Feb 1974.

1131. Brandon Bowman. Born 2 Feb 1977.

1132. Connie Witt. Born 16 Feb 1973 in Harlan County, KY.

Information about the husband and child is from Lombardo.

She married Bert Witt. Born ? . They had the following children:

    1286 i.   Dylan Witt

1133. Tracy Witt. Born 13 Nov 1978.

1134. Stacie Lynn Kelly. Born 15 Jan 1979 in Harlan, KY.

1135. Nevada Terrian Kelly. Born 10 Oct 1982 in Harlan, KY.

1136. Elizabeth Victoria Kelly. Born 15 Jul 1970 in Ypsilanti Washtnaw, MI.

1137. Carmen Stacie Kelly. Born 6 Sep 1971 in Ypsilanti Washtnaw, MI.

1138. Kimberly A. Johnson. Born 8 Aug 1971 in New Rochelle, NY.

1139. Stacie Lynn Johnson. Born 15 Jun 1974 in Connecticut.

1140. William Craig Clark. Born 20 Mar 1970 in Harlan County, KY.

1141. Verlanda Kenona Clark. Born 20 Jun 1973 in Harlan County, KY.

1142. Judel Keturah Clark. Born 3 Jul 1976.

1143. Ronald Witt. Born 7 May 1974 in Pensicola, FL.

1144. Steven Witt. Born 9 May 1978 in Harlan County, KY.

1145. Nicholas Witt. Born 16 Oct 1980 in Harlan County, KY.

1146. Johnny Ray Roberts. Born ? in Alabama.

1147. Edmond Allen Roberts. Born ? in Pennsylvania.

1148. Celia Jean Roberts. Born 31 Jan 1981 in Pennsylvania.

1149. Glen Earl Roberts. Born 11 Feb 1982 in Pennsylvania. Died 28 Dec 1992.

1150. Jasmine Moon Roberts. Born 3 Aug 1985 in Pennsylvania.

1151. Carol Elizabeth Edwards. Born 22 Jul 1955.

1152. Douglas Eugene Witt. Born 8 Mar 1963.

Information about the marriage and children is from Lombardo.

He married Donna Lin Vigo, 29 Sep 1990. Born 8 Mar 1963.

They had the following children:

    1287   i.   Rachelle Witt

    1288   ii.   Jared Douglas Witt

1153. Dean Evan Witt. Born 31 Jan 1960.

Information about the marriage and children is from Lombardo.

He married Laurie Alex Bacigalupi, 28 May 1983. Born 15 Dec 1961. They had the following children:

    1289   i.   David Evan Witt

1290   ii.   Lindsay Ann Witt

1291   iii.   Daniel Edward Witt

1292   iv.   Andrew Gene Witt

1154. Troy Kevin Witt. Born 28 May 1961.

Information about the marriage and children is from Lombardo.

He married Sherri Neuenswander, 6 May 1983. Born 9 Aug 1961. They had the following children:

1293   i.   Jessica Ashley Witt

1294   ii.   Justin Troy Witt

1155. Barry Alan Witt. Born 24 Apr 1962.

Information about the marriage and child is from Lombardo.

He married Denesse Marie May, 14 Feb 1992. Born 4 Nov 1959. They had the following children:

1295   i.   Kelsey Jean Witt

1156. Douglas Scott Witt. Born 17 Jan 1967.

1157. Steven Paul Witt. Born 30 Jul 1968.

1158. Denise Dugger. Born 26 Feb 1965.

1159. Sarah Dugger. Born 7 Feb 1985.

1160. Amy Lynn Witt. Born 9 Apr 1970.

Information about the marriage and children is from Lombardo.

She married Mark Anthony Edwards, 19 Feb 1988. Born 3 Nov 1967. They had the following children:

1296   i.   Mark Anthony Edwards Jr.

1297   ii.   Amber Marie Edwards

1161. Rebecca Kay Witt. Born 1 Nov 1976.

Information about the husband and child is from Lombardo.

She married Ethan Douglas Purcell. Born ? . They had the following children:

1298   i.   Leah Danielle Purcell

1162. Deborah Ann Farley. Born 10 May 1960 in Somerset, KY.

1163. Pamela Jean Farley. Born 4 Jan 1963 in Berea, KY.

1164. Vernon Short. Born 15 Mar 1960.

1165. Joy Gayle Short. Born 20 Sep 1968.

1166. Mike Witt. Born 11 Dec 1964 in Deputy, IN. Died 30 Mar 1972 in Deputy, IN.

1167. Lisa Witt. Born 1 Nov 1968 in Deputy, IN.

Information about the marriage and child is from Lombardo.

She married Jim McCane, 6 May 1989 in Deputy, IN. Born ? .

They had the following children:

        1299   i.   James Adam McCane

1168. Bruce Winston Caudill. Born 16 Mar 1966.

1169. Jerry Caudill. Born 22 Oct 1968 in Harlan County, KY. Died 14 Nov 1987 in Harlan County, KY.

1170. Jerry Howard Caudill. Born 23 Jul 1974 in Harlan County, KY.

1171. Crystal Dianne Caudill. Born 15 Jan 1983.

1172. Christina Messer. Born 4 Jul 1978.

1173. Scott Mayo. Born May 1988.

1174. Jeffrey Craig Witt. Born 28 Aug 1960.

1175. Jennifer Carol Witt. Born 23 Mar 1963.

1176. Janice Crystal Witt. Born 3 Nov 1964.

1177. Tim Poff. Born ? .

1178. Connie Poff. Born ? .

1179. Ronnie Darrell Frazier. Born 12 Oct 1965.

1180. Brian Keith Frazier. Born 9 Jan 1970.

1181. John Christopher Witt. Born 10 Apr 1971.

1182. Tonya Renee Witt. Born 3 Nov 1971.

1183. Sonya Kay Witt. Born 2 Oct 1972.

1184. Angela Kay Witt. Born 2 Jul 1974.

1185. Timothy Wayne Witt. Born 10 Sep 1976.

1186. Delilah Thomas. Born ? .

1187. Beatrice Thomas. Born ? in Harlan County, KY.

1188. Murl Thomas. Born ? in Harlan County, KY.

1189. Toy Thomas. Born ? in Harlan County, KY.

1190. Marty Thomas. Born ? in Harlan County, KY.

1191. Anna Margaret Thomas. Born ? .

1192. Marsha Thomas. Born 5 Dec 1955 in Harlan County, KY.

1193. Steven Dexter Witt. Born 17 Oct 1964 in Scottsburg, IN.
Information about the marriages and children is from Lombardo.

He first married Jenifer Ann McKin, 23 Mar 1986. Born ? . They had the following children:

      1300   i.   Heather Witt

      1301   ii.   Ryan Witt

He second married Susan Matthews, 10 Aug 1996. Born ? .

1194. Brandon Paul Witt. Born 29 Jul 1976 in Louisville, KY.

1195. John Leslie Hildebrand. Born 8 Dec 1982 in Mt. Gilead, OH.

1196. James Jay Hildebrand. Born 23 Aug 1985 in Mt. Gilead, OH.

1197. Sarah Jean Hildebrand. Born 30 Sep 1987 in Mt. Gilead, OH.

1198. Michael Benjamin Witt. Born 12 Nov 1985 in Mt. Gilead, OH.

1199. Nicholas Eric Witt. Born 31 Jan 1991 in Mt. Gilead, OH.

1200. Linda Gail Witt. Born 2 Mar 1958. Died 24 Nov 1959.

1201. Roger Clark Witt. Born 21 Oct 1960.

He married Lisa Berokus, 7 Apr 1981 in Germany. Born ? .
They had the following children:

    1302 i.   April Nicole Witt

    1303 ii.   Jeremy Joesph Witt

    1304 iii.   Melinda Jennette Witt

1202. Ronald Ross Witt. Born 14 Oct 1962 in Cincinnati, OH.

He married Peggy ?, 29 Jul 1981 in Milford, OH. Born ? . They
had the following children:

    1305 i.   Alisha Marie Witt

1203. Linda Marie Witt. Born Circa 1965.

1204. Charles Adrian Witt. Born 28 Aug 1966.

He married ?. Born ? . They had the following children:

    1306 i.   Trevor Witt

1205. Robert Douglas Witt. Born 16 Jun 1970.

He first married Pamela ?. Born ? . They had the following
children:

    1307 i.   Justin Douglas Witt

He second married Valerie ?. Born ? .

1206. Michelle Renee Witt. Born 10 Jan 1972.

1207. Nathan Samuel Witt. Born 13 Jun 1973 in Falmouth, KY.

He married Johnna Ware. Born ? . They had the following
children:

    1308 i.   Jeana Nicole Witt

1208. Megan Rae Clark. Born 12 Mar 1980.

1209. Deems Taylor Gallimore. Born ? . Died ? .

He married Janice ?. Born ? . Died ? .

1210. William Gordon Witt. Born 29 Jul 1941 in Johnson County, IN.

He married Gladys Lucille (Cindy) Wycoff, 19 Jun 1959 in Johnson County, IN. Born 21 Dec 1940. They had the following children:

1309	i.	William Gordon Witt II
1310	ii.	Jefferey Allen Witt
1311	iii.	Timothy Ray Witt
1312	iv.	Pamela Marie Witt

1211. Ronald Clifton Witt. Born 19 Jun 1943 in Johnson, IN.

He married Carolyn Sue Ford, 25 Jun 1961 in Berrien Springs, MI. Born 11 May 1943 in Marion County, IN. They had the following children:

1313	i.	Richard Daniel (Dan) Witt
1314	ii.	Ronald Patrick Witt
1315	iii.	Mark Andrew Witt
1316	iv.	Rebecca Lynn Witt

1212. Kenneth Wayne Witt. Born 7 Dec 1944 in Johnson County, IN.

Kenneth and Mary Burton divorced in 1968; Kenneth adopted Susan Proctor's son, Brian.

He first married Mary (Alice) Burton, 1965 in Franklin, IN. Born Circa 1949. They were divorced. They had the following children:

1317	i.	Teresa Lynn Witt (Reynolds)
1318	ii.	Roberta Jo Witt (Reynolds)

He second married Susan Proctor, Oct 1973 in Franklin, IN. Born 9 Jan 1950. They were divorced. They had the following children:

1319	i.	Brian Proctor Witt

He third married Cindy Ann Courtney, 17 Jun 1989 in Franklin,

IN. Born 10 Jun 1951 in Johnson County, IN.

1213. Stephen Guinnup. Born Circa 1950.

1214. Richard D. Fergason. Born 1 May 1949. Died 5 Mar 1968 in Franklin, IN.

1215. Laura Lee Witt. Born 27 Jun 1959.

She married Paul Randal Woodward, 1978. Born 15 Mar 1958. They had the following children:

    1320 i.   Dillon Randal Woodward

1216. Kevin Matthew Witt. Born 8 Oct 1960.

He first married ?.

He second married Deniece Jarels. Born 24 Oct 1958.

1217. Barry Jay Witt. Born 31 Mar 1962.

He married Deborah Lynn Michaelson. Born 11 Feb 1962. They had the following children:

    1321 i.   Zachery Ryan Witt

1218. Douglas Brian Witt. Born 23 Apr 1964.

He married Lisa Sutherlin. Born Circa 1969. They were divorced. They had the following children:

    1322 i.   Erienne Christine Witt

1219. Craig Allen Witt. Born 12 Jan 1967.

1220. Kristine Kay Witt. Born 1 Jan 1970.

1221. Jonathan Nathan Morris Jr. Born 20 Feb 1963 in Johnson County, IN.

He married Marlene May Cottongim. Born ? .

1222. Gerald Goebel. Born ? .

He married Sue ?. Born ? .

1223. Linda Renee Witt. Born 10 May 1961.

She married Daniel Newberry. Born ? . They had the following children:

    1323 i.   Warren Logan Newberry
    1324 ii.   Garett Cole Newberry

1325   iii.   Katlyn Newberry

1224. Karen Marie Witt. Born 17 Dec 1971.

1225. David Witt. Born Circa 1962.

1226. Randall Wayne Witt. Born 7 Feb 1968 in Cairo, IL.

1227. Julie Ann Witt. Born 31 Dec 1969 in Sikeston, MO.

1228. Donna Kay Witt. Born 30 Nov 1970 in Sikeston, MO.

1229. Tahanna Ann Yeazel. Born 28 Jan 1944.

She married Stanley Schenkel, Circa 1961. Born 24 Oct 1941. Died 30 Apr 1985.

1230. Darrel Duane Yeazel II. Born 7 Oct 1956.

He married Cathline (Cathy) Ortwine, 14 Oct 1976 in Cincinnati, OH. Born 11 Oct 1955 in Cincinnati, OH.

1231. James Robert Witt II. Born 21 Dec 1952.

He married Patty Marie Hughes, 21 Mar 1987 in Frenchtown, IN. Born 8 Jun 1964 in Corydon, IN. They had the following children:

1326   i.   James Robert Witt III
1327   ii.   Emily Marie Witt
1328   iii.   Molly Elizabeth Witt

1232. Jill Stillabower. Born ? .

She married ? Grider. Born ? .

1233. Don Stillabower. Born ? .

He married Rita ?. Born ? .

1234. Roger Witt. Born 3 May 1936.

1235. Joyce Witt. Born 4 Feb 1939.

She married ? Burks. Born ? .

1236. Infant. Born Circa 1939.

1237. Jenette Taylor. Born 4 Feb 1934. Died 5 Feb 1934.

1238. Julia Taylor. Born 4 Feb 1934. Died 5 Feb 1934. Buried in Fair Cemetery.

1239. Pam Taylor. Born 28 Apr 1958 in Springfield, IL.

She married Michael Steven Brady, 30 May 1981 in Edinburg, IL. Born

19 Feb 1951 in New Orleans, LA.

1240. JoAnne Witt. Born 20 Apr 1944 in Casey County, KY. Died 29 Mar 1988 in Casey County, KY.

She married Larry Reed Price, 7 Dec 1963. Born ? . They had the following children:

    1329   i.   Clinton Reed Price

1241. Patsy Dale Patty Witt. Born 6 Dec 1947 in Casey County, KY.

She married Leslie Thomas Dickie Murphy, 18 Dec 1964 in Casey County, KY. Born ? . They had the following children:

    1330   i.   Leah Nicole Murphy

1242. Donna Jean Witt. Born 3 Sep 1947 in Danville, KY.

She first married Harold Price, 18 Apr 1993 in Liberty, KY. Born 14 Jul 1934 in Pricetown, KY.

She second married Dennis Wayne Wesley, 1966. Born 8 Sep 1947 in Liberty, KY. They were divorced. They had the following children:

    1331   i.   Dennis Wayne Wesley II

    1332   ii.   Anthany Ray Wesley

1243. Waunda Lou Witt. Born 27 May 1949 in Danville, KY.

She first married Kenneth Eugene Miller, 23 Oct 1995 in Liberty, KY. Born 21 Feb 1945 in Liberty, KY.

She second married Herman Lester Brown Jr.. Born 23 Jan 1947 in Liberty, KY. They were divorced. They had the following children:

    1333   i.   Steven Boyd Brown

    1334   ii.   Kimberly Dawn Brown

    1335   iii.   Brian Keith Brown

    1336   iv.   David Stuart Brown

    1337   v.   Michael Scott Brown

1244. Larry Ray Witt. Born 3 Dec 1954 in Danville, KY.

He first married Charlotte Queener, 3 Jul 1975 in Barbourville,

KY. Born 1 Dec 1956 in Barbourville, KY. They had the following children:

       1338   i.   Larry Ray Witt II

       1339   ii.   Charlisa Dawn Witt

       1340   iii.   Amberly Martha Witt

He second married Connie Lynn Cassidy, 28 Apr 1984 in Sloans Valley, KY. Born 22 Mar 1965 in Somerset, KY. They had the following children:

       1341   i.   Morgan Matison Witt

1245. Richard Wayne Helm. Born 10 Nov 1945 in Liberty, KY. He first married Mildred Patterson. Born ? .

He second married Linda Fay Lay, 1 Mar 1974 in Liberty, KY. Born 14 Jan 1954 in Casey County, KY.

1246. Jerry Helm. Born 28 Jan 1948 in Liberty, KY.

He married Brenda Vanoy, 3 Sep 1966 in Poplar Grove, Liberty, KY. Born 23 Sep 1947.

1247. Sandra Kay Helm. Born 1 Mar 1956.

She married Billy Ray Martin, Circa 1982. Born ? . They were divorced.

1248. Betty Jean Atwood. Born 4 May 1945 in Jeffersonville, IN. She married Dale Herrin. Born ? .

1249. Linda Sue Atwood. Born 27 Aug 1947 in Casey County She married Herman Dwayne Atwood, in Casey County, KY. Born ? .

1250. Charlene Witt. Born 30 Aug 1953 in Hamilton County, OH. She married Noble Tucker, 25 Sep 1970 in Covington, KY. Born 14 Jun 1950 in McCreary County, KY. They had the following children:

       1342   i.   Tracy Lynette Tucker

       1343   ii.   Noble Shane Tucker

1251. Francine Witt. Born 5 Jan 1955.

She first married Rudy Allen, 24 Nov 1976 in Hamilton, OH. Born 1956. They were divorced 1980. They had the following children:

    1344   i.   Darla Nicole (Niki) Allen

    1345   ii.   Shawn Luther Allen

She second married Richard Hacker, 6 Jan 1981 in Hamilton, OH. Born 14 Jul 1945 in Stanford, KY.

1252. Annette Witt. Born 15 Feb 1956.

She married Ronald Isaacs, 8 Nov 1971 in Evandale, OH. Born 26 Jan 1949. They had the following children:

    1346   i.   Ronda Ann Isaacs

    1347   ii.   Tonya Isaacs

    1348   iii.   Ronald Isaacs Jr.

1253. Denise Witt. Born 13 Feb 1963 in Cincinnati, OH.

She married Wilbure Edward Witt, 31 Aug 1983 in Hamilton, OH. Born 14 Jan 1963 in Cincinnati, OH. They were divorced 7 Feb 1994. They had the following children:

    1349   i.   Wilbure Edward Witt Jr.

    1350   ii.   Luther Zachiaria Witt

    1351   iii.   Benjamin Isiah Witt

1254. Teresa Witt. Born 22 May 1964 in Cincinnati, OH.

She married Dennis Lee Oldsield, 16 Apr 1983 in Cincinnati, OH. Born 2 Sep 1962 in Cincinnati, OH. They had the following children:

    1352   i.   Jacob Lee Oldsield

    1353   ii.   Joshua Ray Oldsield

1255. James Nelson Jeffries. Born ? .

1256. Glenda Gail Jeffries. Born ? .

1257. Girl Jeffries. Born ? .

1258. Carlis Dean Witt. Born 21 Oct 1936 in Casey County, KY.

He married Geraldean Jean Shoopman, Circa 1960 in Casey

County, KY. Born Circa 1941. They had the following children:

    1354   i.   Deadra Witt

1259. Mona Carol Witt. Born 6 Jan 1941.

    She married Kenneth Wesley Stafford, 1 Jan 1957 in Casey County, KY. Born 2 Apr 1938 in Casey County, KY. They had the following children:

    1355   i.   Greg Vincent Stafford

1260. Dorotha Sue Witt. Born 23 Dec 1945.

    She married Paul Allen Hatter, 13 Mar 1963 in Livingston, TN. Born 30 Nov 1945 in Boyle County, KY. They had the following children:

    1356   i.   Terry Allen Hatter

    1357   ii.   Jefferey Allen Hatter

1261. Bobby Sherill Lynn. Born 19 Jul 1936 in Casey County, KY.

    He married Marketia Ann LaFavers, 15 Mar 1955 in Casey County, KY. Born Circa 1938. Died Circa 1996.

1262. Wanda Lou Lynn. Born 5 Nov 1939.

    She married Richard Waltz. Born ? .

1263. Dana Marc (Danny) Rullo. Born 17 Jun 1947.

1264. Patty Witt. Born Circa 1947.

1265. Linda Witt. Born Circa 1949.

1266. Belinda Gail Witt. Born 1 Oct 1951. Died ? . Buried in Antioch Christian Church Cemetery.

1267. Jill Witt. Born 18 Apr 1953.

    She married Joe R. Johnson III. Born ? . They were divorced. They had the following children:

    1358   i.   Daniel Craig Johnson

    1359   ii.   Christin Page Johnson

    1360   iii.   Philip Seth Johnson

1268. Gina Lynn Witt. Born 13 Nov 1965.

She first married Ray Manning, Circa 1983 in Stanford, KY.
Born ? . They were divorced. They had the following children:

    1361   i.   Krista Manning

    1362   ii.   Shana Ray Manning

She second married Jerry Lynn, Circa 1992 in Stanford, KY.
Born ? .

1269. Steven Ray Wilson. Born 30 Aug 1953.

He married Christia Wiss. Born ? .

1270. Wendy Paige Atwood. Born 22 May 1973.

She married Ryan Tyler Howard, 21 Dec 1995. Born ? .

1271. Robyn Renee Atwood. Born 24 Oct 1976.

1272. Kevin Dewayne Witt. Born 13 Apr 1963 in Glasgow, KY.

He first married Penny Renee Hunt, daughter of Jimmy Hunt &
Brenda Wheet, 15 Mar 1985 in Allen County, KY. Born ? .

He second married Tonda Minix, daughter of Cecil Minix &
Anita Douglas, 18 May 1991 in Allen County, KY. Born ? .

1273. Tonya Allen. Born 13 Aug 1975.

1274. Billy J. Miller. Born 8 Nov 1973.

1275. Alicia Byrn. Born 20 Aug 1983.

1276. Jacqueline N. Brown. Born 5 Oct 1962 in Allen County,
KY.

1277. Charles F. Brown. Born 4 Apr 1964 in Allen County, KY.

1278. Hugh B. Brown. Born 27 Feb 1967 in Allen County, KY.

1279. Deborah Willoughby. Born 8 Sep 1963.

1280. Laurie Willoughby. Born 3 Jan 1973.

1281. Joshua S. Witt. Born 23 Dec 1986 in Barren County, KY.

1282. Chad Carter. Born 15 Jul 1983 in Allen County, KY.

1283. Holly Carter. Born Apr 1987 in Allen County, KY.

1284. James M. Barton. Born 8 Feb 1974 in Allen County, KY.

1285. Amber Witt. Born ? .

1286. **Dylan Witt.** Born ? .

1287. **Rachelle Witt.** Born 27 Dec 1991.

1288. **Jared Douglas Witt.** Born 27 Dec 1991.

1289. **David Evan Witt.** Born 12 Apr 1984.

1290. **Lindsay Ann Witt.** Born 6 Jul 1986.

1291. **Daniel Edward Witt.** Born 19 Apr 1988.

1292. **Andrew Gene Witt.** Born 6 Jun 1993.

1293. **Jessica Ashley Witt.** Born 9 Mar 1986.

1294. **Justin Troy Witt.** Born 22 Jul 1990.

1295. **Kelsey Jean Witt.** Born 19 Jul 1992.

1296. **Mark Anthony Edwards Jr.** Born 24 Mar 1989.

1297. **Amber Marie Edwards.** Born 15 Aug 1991.

1298. **Leah Danielle Purcell.** Born 7 Jan 1994.

1299. **James Adam McCane.** Born 3 May 1993.

1300. **Heather Witt.** Born 29 Jul 1986.

1301. **Ryan Witt.** Born 2 May 1988.

1302. **April Nicole Witt.** Born 4 Jan 1983.

1303. **Jeremy Joesph Witt.** Born 27 Aug 1985.

1304. **Melinda Jennette Witt.** Born 10 Aug 1986.

1305. **Alisha Marie Witt.** Born 16 Mar 1983.

1306. **Trevor Witt.** Born 26 Dec 1989.

1307. **Justin Douglas Witt.** Born 5 Feb 1989.

1308. **Jeana Nicole Witt.** Born 12 Jun 1991.

1309. **William Gordon Witt II.** Born 6 Dec 1959 in Johnson County, IN.

He first married Paula Bates, Circa 1982 in Indianapolis, IN. Born 2 Nov 1954. They were divorced. They had the following children:

    1363 i.   Lindsey Leigh Witt

He second married Jody Diane Ehman, About 1991 in Indianapolis, IN. Born 25 Sep 1970. They had the following children:

    1364 i.   Boy Witt

1310. **Jefferey Allen Witt.** Born 5 Dec 1960.

1311. **Timothy Ray Witt.** Born 30 Dec 1961.

1312. **Pamela Marie Witt.** Born 30 Mar 1964.

1313. **Richard Daniel (Dan) Witt.** Born 14 May 1962.

1314. **Ronald Patrick Witt.** Born 5 Apr 1964.

1315. **Mark Andrew Witt.** Born 9 Apr 1965.

1316. **Rebecca Lynn Witt.** Born 5 Nov 1967.

1317. **Teresa Lynn Witt (Reynolds).** Born 19 Jul 1967.

1318. **Roberta Jo Witt (Reynolds).** Born 31 Jul 1965.

She married Randal Camp, 1988 in Florida. Born ? .

1319. **Brian Proctor Witt.** Born 16 Apr 1971.

1320. **Dillon Randal Woodward.** Born 27 Sep 1991.

1321. **Zachery Ryan Witt.** Born 6 Dec 1984.

1322. **Erienne Christine Witt.** Born Circa 1990.

1323. **Warren Logan Newberry.** Born About 1991.

1324. **Garett Cole Newberry.** Born 28 Dec 1993.

1325. **Katlyn Newberry.** Born 5 Feb 1996.

1326. **James Robert Witt III.** Born 30 Aug 1987.

1327. **Emily Marie Witt.** Born 15 Jan 1989.

1328. **Molly Elizabeth Witt.** Born 2 Apr 1992.

1329. **Clinton Reed Price.** Born 26 Jul 1964.
   He married Paula Buck. Born ? .

1330. **Leah Nicole Murphy.** Born 17 Jun 1970 in Danville, KY.
   She married William Wethington. Born ? .

1331. **Dennis Wayne Wesley II.** Born 18 Apr 1966.
   He married Vicki Jean Terrell, 12 Jun 1992 in Alums Springs,
KY. Born 19 Jul 1965.

1332. **Anthany Ray Wesley.** Born 15 Dec 1969.

1333. **Steven Boyd Brown.** Born 10 Nov 1964.
   He married Rhonda Kay Clark. Born Circa 1966.

1334. **Kimberly Dawn Brown.** Born 26 Oct 1965.

1335. **Brian Keith Brown.** Born 8 May 1970.

1336. **David Stuart Brown.** Born 22 Apr 1971.

1337. **Michael Scott Brown.** Born 28 Jan 1973.
   He married Andrea Lee Harris. Born 22 Mar 1973 in
McMinville, TN.

1338. **Larry Ray Witt II.** Born 17 Apr 1978 in Danville, KY.

1339. **Charlisa Dawn Witt.** Born 29 Aug 1982.

1340. **Amberly Martha Witt.** Born 21 Sep 1983.

1341. **Morgan Matison Witt.** Born 2 Apr 1997 in Somerset, KY.

1342. **Tracy Lynette Tucker.** Born 21 Jan 1971.

1343. **Noble Shane Tucker.** Born 14 Apr 1980.

1344. **Darla Nicole (Niki) Allen.** Born 17 May 1974.

1345. Shawn Luther Allen. Born 17 May 1977.

1346. Ronda Ann Isaacs. Born 4 Mar 1972.

She married Clifford Lewis Nuce, 25 Jun 1994 in Westchester, OH. Born ? .

1347. Tonya Isaacs. Born 29 Nov 1973.

She married Chris McPhail, 16 Sep 1994. Born ? .

1348. Ronald Isaacs Jr. Born 22 May 1977.

1349. Wilbure Edward Witt Jr. Born 17 Oct 1984.

1350. Luther Zachiaria Witt. Born 2 Jan 1988.

1351. Benjamin Isiah Witt. Born 3 Feb 1989.

1352. Jacob Lee Oldsield. Born 8 Dec 1984.

1353. Joshua Ray Oldsield. Born 17 Oct 1986.

1354. Deadra Witt. Born Circa 1962.

She married Harold Cochron. Born ? .

1355. Greg Vincent Stafford. Born 22 Nov 1958 in Casey County, KY.

He first married Carla Reed, 2 Feb 1985 in Lincoln County, KY. Born 11 Nov 1965 in Lincoln County, KY.

He second married Martha Sue McDonald. Born ? .

1356. Terry Allen Hatter. Born 20 Jul 1963 in Boyle County, KY.

He married Rhonda Louise Vaught, 19 Oct 1985 in Livingston, TN. Born 26 Jan 1966.

1357. Jefferey Allen Hatter. Born 25 May 1969 in Boyle County, KY.

He married Sylvia Marie Black, 18 Jun 1988 in Casey County, KY. Born 12 Nov 1970.

1358. Daniel Craig Johnson. Born 28 Jan 1974.

He married Paula ?. Born ? .

1359. Christin Page Johnson. Born 17 Dec 1977.

1360. Philip Seth Johnson. Born 4 Jul 1979.

1361. Krista Manning. Born 15 Jan 1984.

1362. Shana Ray Manning. Born 4 Mar 1991.

1363. **Lindsey Leigh Witt.** Born 21 Feb 1983.
1364. **Boy Witt.** Born Circa 1992.

Index

Hill, Carl	861	Jeffries, Girl	1257
Hill, Charles Marvin	858	Jeffries, Glenda Gail	1256
Hill, Clementine	863	Jeffries, James Nelson	1255
Hill, Dorotha	865	Johnson, Christin Page	1359
Hill, Edmonston	862	Johnson, Daniel Craig	1358
Hill, Jack	866	Johnson, Kimberly A.	1138
Hill, Lucille	859	Johnson, Philip Seth	1360
Hill, Muriel	864	Johnson, Stacie Lynn	1139
Hill, Ruby	860	Kelly, Ballard Jr.	769
Hix, Daniel	880	Kelly, Carmen Stacie	1137
Hix, Janie	879	Kelly, Clayton Odell	978
Hix, Susie Bell	882	Kelly, David Bradley	982
Hix, Witt	881	Kelly, Elizabeth Victoria	1136
Holmes, Celia	775	Kelly, Mildred Sue	979
Holmes, Comrad	778	Kelly, Nevada Terrian	1135
Holmes, Delonia	774	Kelly, Stacie Lynn	1134
Holmes, Edgar	772	Kelly, Teresa Mary	980
Holmes, Flossie	770	Kelly, Tina Renaee	981
Holmes, Glenda	771	Key, Barbary	58
Holmes, Kermit	777	Key, Elizabeth	57
Holmes, Lana	776	Key, George	63
Holmes, Wilmer	773	Key, John Waller	62
Howard, Connie Ann	996	Key, Joseph	64
Howard, Earl Jr.	997	Key, Judith	59
Howard, John Terry	998	Key, William	61
Howard, Ricky Darrel	995	Key, Winney	60
Huddlesey, Adler	127	King, Hazel	804
Huddlesey, Adonijah	126	Lain, Ben W.	604
Huddlesey, Charles	123	Lain, C. Cissa	602
Huddlesey, Elizabeth	128	Lain, Charles J.	601
Huddlesey, James Jennius	122	Lain, Frances C.	598
Huddlesey, Jesse	125	Lain, Jo M.	603
Huddlesey, Parthenia	124	Lain, John W.	599
Huff, Cassie	767	Lain, Mary A.	600
Huff, Cheryl Darlene	991	Linville, Cara	1117
Huff, Ferrell	768	Linville, Sam Jr.	1116
Huff, Linda	990	Lynn, Bobby Sherill	1261
Huff, Ronald J.	989	Lynn, Wanda Lou	1262
Hunt, Jesse	1119	Manning, Krista	1361
Hunt, Orville	1118	Manning, Shana Ray	1362
Infant,	1236	Martin, Constance	695
Infant,	624	Martin, Dicie	692
Isaacs, Ronald Jr.	1348	Martin, Lucy	691
Isaacs, Ronda Ann	1346	Martin, Mildred	693
Isaacs, Tonya	1347	Martin, Nancy	694
Jarnigan, Jeremide	186	Mayo, Scott	1173

Varner, James J.	409	Witt, Allen	394
Varner, John	412	Witt, Allenson	238
Varner, Mary Alabama	410	Witt, Allie	679
Varner, Nancy Ann	408	Witt, Almer	833
Varner, Sarah	411	Witt, Almira	231
Varner, Sophronia	414	Witt, Almyra	406
Wells, Cecil Ambrose	1071	Witt, Alnier	828
Wells, Hazel Margaret	1072	Witt, Alonzo K.	677
Wells, Mildred Marie	1073	Witt, Alpha	802
Wells, Richard Eugene	1074	Witt, Alpha E.	533
Wells, Samuel Estill Jr.	1075	Witt, Alton	806
Wesley, Anthany Ray	1332	Witt, Amanda	435
Wesley, Dennis Wayne II	1331	Witt, Amber	1285
Whitney, James	1086	Witt, Amberly Martha	1340
Whitney, Nellie	1085	Witt, Ambrose	336
Whitney, Willie Louise	1096	Witt, Amelia	379
Willoughby, Deborah	1279	Witt, Amey	71
Willoughby, Laurie	1280	Witt, Amy Lynn	1160
Wilson, Steven Ray	1269	Witt, Anderson	363
Witt (Reynolds), Roberta Jo	1318	Witt, Andrew	353
Witt (Reynolds), Teresa L,	1317	Witt, Andrew Gene	1292
Witt, ?	10	Witt, Andrew Jackson	333
Witt, ?	11	Witt, Andrew Jackson	376
Witt, ?	223	Witt, Andrew Jackson	568
Witt, ?	629	Witt, Andrew Jessie	959
Witt, Abigail	294	Witt, Andy Lee	758
Witt, Abijah	77	Witt, Andy Lee Jr.	939
Witt, Abner	140	Witt, Angela Kay	1184
Witt, Abner	145	Witt, Ann	116
Witt, Abner	45	Witt, Ann	143
Witt, Abner Lewis	229	Witt, Ann	228
Witt, Ada	798	Witt, Ann S.	271
Witt, Ada	829	Witt, Ann Sparks	164
Witt, Adell	836	Witt, Anna	327
Witt, Adoline	389	Witt, Anna Pearl	656
Witt, Adolphus (Dof)	417	Witt, Anne	17
Witt, Agnes	15	Witt, Annette	1252
Witt, Aires	85	Witt, Annie Kirk	733
Witt, Alabama	402	Witt, Anthony	91
Witt, Albert	830	Witt, Anthony Jr	179
Witt, Alex	576	Witt, April Nicole	1302
Witt, Alfred	310	Witt, Arcelia	948
Witt, Alice	386	Witt, Archable	349
Witt, Alice G.	597	Witt, Archibald	177
Witt, Alisha Marie	1305	Witt, Archibald	312
Witt, Allen	241	Witt, Archibald	548

Witt, Archibald	76	Witt, Burgess	84
Witt, Archie Ercil	971	Witt, Caleb	110
Witt, Arla Louise	1062	Witt, Camden Hezikiah	511
Witt, Arlis Edward	1063	Witt, Candice (Dicie)	515
Witt, Armaina	984	Witt, Capernia	714
Witt, Arthur	815	Witt, Carlis Dean	1258
Witt, Asa	453	Witt, Carol Ann	968
Witt, Asa William	484	Witt, Carolyn Lou	1015
Witt, Aubrey G.	909	Witt, Carolyn Lou	1124
Witt, Aubrey Wilson	924	Witt, Carrie	652
Witt, Audra	1019	Witt, Carrie E.	541
Witt, Audrey	841	Witt, Carrie Nell	911
Witt, Barnie Merle	985	Witt, Catherine (Kittie)	269
Witt, Barry Alan	1155	Witt, Catherine H.	377
Witt, Barry Jay	1217	Witt, Cecil	725
Witt, Barthena	465	Witt, Cecil Eugene	1078
Witt, Belinda Gail	1266	Witt, Cecilia	167
Witt, Benjamin	13	Witt, Celeste	622
Witt, Benjamin F.	371	Witt, Celia A.	556
Witt, Benjamin F.	592	Witt, Charity	105
Witt, Benjamin Isiah	1351	Witt, Charlene	1250
Witt, Benjamin J.	458	Witt, Charles	138
Witt, Benjamin Jr.	53	Witt, Charles	144
Witt, Benny	1039	Witt, Charles	217
Witt, Bernice	1077	Witt, Charles	362
Witt, Bertha	1025	Witt, Charles	403
Witt, Bertha M.	779	Witt, Charles	42
Witt, Bessie	1016	Witt, Charles	46
Witt, Bessie	585	Witt, Charles	502
Witt, Bessie Kathryn	1064	Witt, Charles	55
Witt, Bessie Lee	661	Witt, Charles	839
Witt, Bettie	713	Witt, Charles	90
Witt, Bettie D.	498	Witt, Charles	908
Witt, Betty Lois	1024	Witt, Charles Adrian	1204
Witt, Betty Rosetta	976	Witt, Charles Foster	375
Witt, Betty Ruth	1051	Witt, Charles Horner	202
Witt, Betty Sue	1080	Witt, Charles L.	398
Witt, Beulah	797	Witt, Charles Lewis	423
Witt, Beulah	842	Witt, Charles Lon	709
Witt, Billy O'Neal	943	Witt, Charles R.	760
Witt, Billy O'Neal Jr.	1125	Witt, Charles Robert	1094
Witt, Boy	1066	Witt, Charles Sherman	614
Witt, Boy	1364	Witt, Charles Sherman II	1049
Witt, Brandon Paul	1194	Witt, Charles W.	1104
Witt, Brian Proctor	1319	Witt, Charles Wylie	141
Witt, Burgess	170	Witt, Charles Wylie Jr.	237

Witt, Charley	477	Witt, David H.	448
Witt, Charlie	688	Witt, David H.	496
Witt, Charlie M.	500	Witt, David III	278
Witt, Charlisa Dawn	1339	Witt, David Jr.	165
Witt, Chelf	421	Witt, David Nelson	460
Witt, Chester	791	Witt, David William	381
Witt, Chester Roy	963	Witt, Deadra	1354
Witt, Child	315	Witt, Dean	438
Witt, Clabe	478	Witt, Dean Evan	1153
Witt, Clarence Lee	1050	Witt, Delaney	248
Witt, Claude	831	Witt, Delaney Jr.	476
Witt, Clayborn	445	Witt, Della	826
Witt, Cleo Elizabeth	967	Witt, Delmas	584
Witt, Clercia	794	Witt, Denise	1253
Witt, Clifton	1017	Witt, Dennet	163
Witt, Clinton	687	Witt, Dennet Abner	486
Witt, Clyde	821	Witt, Denny	1037
Witt, Clyde II	1035	Witt, Dice (Candice)	169
Witt, Coleman	207	Witt, Dicie	268
Witt, Connie	1132	Witt, Dillard	1076
Witt, Connie	489	Witt, Dillard	780
Witt, Cory Edward	934	Witt, Dillard Douglas	964
Witt, Craig Allen	1219	Witt, Docia	534
Witt, Curtis	819	Witt, Donna Jean	1242
Witt, Cynthia	328	Witt, Donna Kay	1228
Witt, Cynthia	344	Witt, Donnie Ray	977
Witt, Cynthia	443	Witt, Dora	174
Witt, Dana J.	1106	Witt, Dorotha Sue	1260
Witt, Daniel	192	Witt, Dorothy A.	1105
Witt, Daniel	559	Witt, Dorothy Virginia	1027
Witt, Daniel	728	Witt, Douglas Brian	1218
Witt, Daniel Edward	1291	Witt, Douglas Eugene	1152
Witt, Daniel Kirk	512	Witt, Douglas Scott	1156
Witt, Darrell Willard	1013	Witt, Dovie	945
Witt, Darshall	946	Witt, Duskie Delores	972
Witt, Dave	920	Witt, Dwight H.	1110
Witt, David	1043	Witt, Dylan	1286
Witt, David	1225	Witt, Earl	785
Witt, David	149	Witt, Earl	840
Witt, David	275	Witt, Earl	930
Witt, David	283	Witt, Earl Edmond	796
Witt, David	301	Witt, Earl Edmond Jr.	954
Witt, David	41	Witt, Earl Omer	663
Witt, David	50	Witt, Earnest Clyde	543
Witt, David	89	Witt, Edgar	823
Witt, David Evan	1289	Witt, Edgar Howard	1055

Witt, Edgar Jr.	1044	Witt, Elizabeth Jane	1041
Witt, Edgar Kennedy	546	Witt, Ellen	396
Witt, Edily Florence	761	Witt, Ellen	468
Witt, Edith Lanere	1053	Witt, Elnora	232
Witt, Edmond	175	Witt, Elvada	555
Witt, Edmond	326	Witt, Emalin	243
Witt, Edmund	25	Witt, Emaline	471
Witt, Edmund	550	Witt, Emeline	331
Witt, Edmund	78	Witt, Emeline	358
Witt, Edmund Jr.	92	Witt, Emily (?)	427
Witt, Edna Cleo	944	Witt, Emily J.	593
Witt, Edna May	925	Witt, Emily M.	378
Witt, Edward	1067	Witt, Emily Marie	1327
Witt, Edward	355	Witt, Emma Jane	664
Witt, Edward	4	Witt, Enoch	203
Witt, Eggy	98	Witt, Erienne Christine	1322
Witt, Elbridge	708	Witt, Ernest Yerkes	668
Witt, Eleanor G.	726	Witt, Ethel	832
Witt, Eli	190	Witt, Eugene	483
Witt, Eli	338	Witt, Eugene Kennon	671
Witt, Elijah	104	Witt, Evelyn	1045
Witt, Elisha	48	Witt, Evelyn	928
Witt, Elisha Berry	156	Witt, Everett	905
Witt, Elisha Jr.	146	Witt, Everette Wayne	1089
Witt, Eliza	281	Witt, Fannie	385
Witt, Eliza	384	Witt, Fannie	473
Witt, Eliza A	428	Witt, Fannie	583
Witt, Eliza J.	616	Witt, Flora Bell	627
Witt, Eliza Kate	540	Witt, Flora Grace	560
Witt, Elizabeth	131	Witt, Florence	513
Witt, Elizabeth	132	Witt, Floyd Winston	938
Witt, Elizabeth	182	Witt, Forest	848
Witt, Elizabeth	199	Witt, Frances J.	285
Witt, Elizabeth	306	Witt, Francine	1251
Witt, Elizabeth	350	Witt, Francis	467
Witt, Elizabeth	357	Witt, Fred	783
Witt, Elizabeth	366	Witt, Gardner R.	662
Witt, Elizabeth	392	Witt, Garfield	571
Witt, Elizabeth	454	Witt, Garland	246
Witt, Elizabeth	681	Witt, General Marion	554
Witt, Elizabeth	73	Witt, Geneva Charity	799
Witt, Elizabeth	80	Witt, Geneva L.	1113
Witt, Elizabeth	849	Witt, George	240
Witt, Elizabeth "Betsy"	152	Witt, George	47
Witt, Elizabeth (Bessie)	1068	Witt, George D.	501
Witt, Elizabeth B.	419	Witt, George Everett	903

Witt, George H.	650	Witt, Infant	545
Witt, George R.	456	Witt, Ira G.	345
Witt, George W.	703	Witt, Isaac	325
Witt, George Wallace	1056	Witt, Isaac N. V.	558
Witt, Georgia	942	Witt, Isaiah	447
Witt, Georgia Fay	845	Witt, Issac N.	480
Witt, Gibson	227	Witt, J. C.	935
Witt, Gina Lynn	1268	Witt, J. C.	974
Witt, Ginna	393	Witt, Jackie R.	1109
Witt, Glen Curtis	1028	Witt, Jacob	347
Witt, Gordon Burgess	729	Witt, James	201
Witt, Grant	782	Witt, James	213
Witt, Gwen	809	Witt, James	244
Witt, H. M.	474	Witt, James	284
Witt, Hannah	114	Witt, James	351
Witt, Hannah	37	Witt, James	401
Witt, Haran Edmond	955	Witt, James	586
Witt, Harlen Ray	789	Witt, James	822
Witt, Harlin G.	923	Witt, James	93
Witt, Harmon	191	Witt, James Callie	619
Witt, Harold	628	Witt, James D.	337
Witt, Hattie	689	Witt, James D.	420
Witt, Hattie Lenora	665	Witt, James E.	1026
Witt, Hazen Hurst	544	Witt, James E.	721
Witt, Heather	1300	Witt, James F.	705
Witt, Helen Ailene	1020	Witt, James H.	230
Witt, Helen Dean	1103	Witt, James H.	436
Witt, Henri Ella	707	Witt, James H.	547
Witt, Henry	96	Witt, James Letcher	706
Witt, Henry Clayton	461	Witt, James M.	250
Witt, Henry T.	549	Witt, James M.	451
Witt, Herbert Louis	1031	Witt, James M.	536
Witt, Herman	820	Witt, James Monroe	539
Witt, Herschell H.	711	Witt, James Robert	1038
Witt, Hester Jane	459	Witt, James Robert II	1231
Witt, Hester Jane	649	Witt, James Robert III	1326
Witt, Hezekiah	22	Witt, James S.	1054
Witt, Hezekiah	300	Witt, James William	648
Witt, Hezekiah	74	Witt, Jane	224
Witt, Hezikiah	292	Witt, Jane	364
Witt, Homer Birchel	960	Witt, Janice Crystal	1176
Witt, Howard	790	Witt, Janie L.	1108
Witt, Hubert	580	Witt, Jared Douglas	1288
Witt, Ida J.	759	Witt, Jarusha	368
Witt, India Mae	904	Witt, Jasper Franklin	316
Witt, Inez Wavolene	975	Witt, Jeana Nicole	1308

Witt, Jeanie	119	Witt, John	54
Witt, Jefferey Allen	1310	Witt, John	605
Witt, Jefferson	441	Witt, John	704
Witt, Jeffrey Craig	1174	Witt, John	94
Witt, Jeffrey Scott	1111	Witt, John A.	430
Witt, Jemmie	900	Witt, John B. Floyd	537
Witt, Jennifer Carol	1175	Witt, John Carter	788
Witt, Jenny	986	Witt, John Christopher	1181
Witt, Jeremy	1129	Witt, John E.	282
Witt, Jeremy Joesph	1303	Witt, John F.	509
Witt, Jerimah	390	Witt, John H.	538
Witt, Jesse	120	Witt, John H.	901
Witt, Jesse	133	Witt, John III ~	134
Witt, Jesse	226	Witt, John III _	9
Witt, Jesse	39	Witt, John IV ~	35
Witt, Jesse	452	Witt, John Jr.	2
Witt, Jesse	631	Witt, John Jr.	44
Witt, Jesse	88	Witt, John Jr.	65
Witt, Jesse David	485	Witt, John Larry	1088
Witt, Jessica Ashley	1293	Witt, John M.	251
Witt, Jill	1267	Witt, John M.	518
Witt, Jincy	253	Witt, John P.	220
Witt, JoAnne	1240	Witt, John P.	233
Witt, Joe A. P.	657	Witt, John Q.	653
Witt, John	1	Witt, John R.	382
Witt, John	113	Witt, John Silas	551
Witt, John	12	Witt, John V	117
Witt, John	150	Witt, John V.	439
Witt, John	153	Witt, John W.	291
Witt, John	172	Witt, John W.	455
Witt, John	18	Witt, John W.	678
Witt, John	189	Witt, John Wesley	528
Witt, John	212	Witt, John Wesley	569
Witt, John	225	Witt, Jonathan	181
Witt, John	23	Witt, Joseph	111
Witt, John	266	Witt, Joseph Henry	675
Witt, John	297	Witt, Joseph Jr.	208
Witt, John	309	Witt, Joseph King	1012
Witt, John	329	Witt, Josepha	462
Witt, John	361	Witt, Josephine Cornelia	514
Witt, John	369	Witt, Joshua	82
Witt, John	395	Witt, Joshua S.	1281
Witt, John	407	Witt, Joyce	1235
Witt, John	450	Witt, Joyce	40
Witt, John	487	Witt, Judah	38
Witt, John	504	Witt, Julia Ann	373

Witt, Julia Marie	957	Witt, Lindsay Ann	1290
Witt, Julie Ann	1227	Witt, Lindsey Leigh	1363
Witt, Juliet	953	Witt, Linnie	168
Witt, Justin Douglas	1307	Witt, Lisa	1167
Witt, Justin Troy	1294	Witt, Lisa Dianne	1112
Witt, Karen Marie	1224	Witt, Littleberry	221
Witt, Kathlene	850	Witt, Littlebury	155
Witt, Keith	1128	Witt, Littlebury	43
Witt, Kelsey Jean	1295	Witt, Littlebury	6
Witt, Kenneth Wayne	1212	Witt, Lizzie	919
Witt, Kevin Dewayne	1272	Witt, Lon P.	724
Witt, Kevin Matthew	1216	Witt, Lonnie Dale	1030
Witt, Kizzie Ann	527	Witt, Lora	623
Witt, Kristine Kay	1220	Witt, Loran D.	1036
Witt, Laminia	499	Witt, Lorene	838
Witt, Lareca	1091	Witt, Louella	898
Witt, Larry Ray	1244	Witt, Louisa Ann	469
Witt, Larry Ray II	1338	Witt, Louisa J.	242
Witt, Latticia	335	Witt, Louise	807
Witt, Laura	618	Witt, Lousinda	247
Witt, Laura	719	Witt, Lousinda Burilla	482
Witt, Laura Lee	1215	Witt, Louvinia J.	463
Witt, Lavinia	102	Witt, Lucille	933
Witt, Lavinia J.	352	Witt, Lucy	154
Witt, Lawrence	792	Witt, Lucy	51
Witt, Lawretta	701	Witt, Lucy	718
Witt, Lee Ella	659	Witt, Lucy Ellen	383
Witt, Lela M. (Marie?)	1057	Witt, Lucy Fay	846
Witt, Leman	572	Witt, Lucy M.	594
Witt, Lenna Clay	670	Witt, Lula	712
Witt, Leonard H.	589	Witt, Lula Mabel	1048
Witt, Leonard L.	762	Witt, Luther	824
Witt, Leonard Raymond	669	Witt, Luther H.	510
Witt, Leslie Green	817	Witt, Luther Jr.	1061
Witt, Leta Oneda	1029	Witt, Luther Zachiaria	1350
Witt, Levina E.	433	Witt, Lydia	107
Witt, Lewis	56	Witt, Mack	683
Witt, Lewis	87	Witt, Madie	727
Witt, Lillian	847	Witt, Magaline	927
Witt, Lillie Lavonne	956	Witt, Malie Emma	672
Witt, Lillie May	851	Witt, Malinda	267
Witt, Lily May	1034	Witt, Malrinda	249
Witt, Linda	1265	Witt, Margaret	137
Witt, Linda Gail	1200	Witt, Margaret	160
Witt, Linda Marie	1203	Witt, Margaret	314
Witt, Linda Renee	1223	Witt, Margaret	690

Witt, Margaret Ann	1090	Witt, Mary Kathleen	731
Witt, Margaret Brand	734	Witt, Mateson M.	388
Witt, Margaret Helen	907	Witt, Matilda (Tillie)	621
Witt, Maria E.	418	Witt, Mattie	685
Witt, Marianne Jr.	52	Witt, Maud Ella	660
Witt, Marietta	612	Witt, Maude	582
Witt, Mark Andrew	1315	Witt, Maude Elizabeth	730
Witt, Martha	194	Witt, Maurice	916
Witt, Martha	239	Witt, Max	1018
Witt, Martha	313	Witt, May	245
Witt, Martha	330	Witt, Mayme	655
Witt, Martha	339	Witt, McClellan	470
Witt, Martha	69	Witt, Melinda Jennette	1304
Witt, Martha C.	432	Witt, Melissa A.	422
Witt, Martha Elizabeth F.	506	Witt, Melville Lee	676
Witt, Martha Jane	532	Witt, Mendy	581
Witt, Martha Jane	552	Witt, Merrill	206
Witt, Martin Harrington	178	Witt, Michael Benjamin	1198
Witt, Marvin	921	Witt, Michael Eric	1000
Witt, Mary	103	Witt, Michelle Renee	1206
Witt, Mary	118	Witt, Middy	16
Witt, Mary	135	Witt, Mike	1166
Witt, Mary	20	Witt, Milda	464
Witt, Mary	219	Witt, Mildred	112
Witt, Mary	332	Witt, Mildred	837
Witt, Mary	342	Witt, Mildred	926
Witt, Mary	36	Witt, Mildred Fleenor	941
Witt, Mary	387	Witt, Mildred Jr	159
Witt, Mary	391	Witt, Mildred Opal	1058
Witt, Mary	404	Witt, Miles	531
Witt, Mary	573	Witt, Millie	129
Witt, Mary	72	Witt, Mindy	575
Witt, Mary "Polly"	162	Witt, Molly Elizabeth	1328
Witt, Mary (Polly)	236	Witt, Mona Carol	1259
Witt, Mary A.	400	Witt, Morgan Matison	1341
Witt, Mary A.	416	Witt, Mourning	210
Witt, Mary A.	535	Witt, Myrtle	666
Witt, Mary Ann	311	Witt, Myrtle	834
Witt, Mary Ann	360	Witt, Nancy	1042
Witt, Mary Ann	553	Witt, Nancy	218
Witt, Mary E.	1060	Witt, Nancy	273
Witt, Mary E.	431	Witt, Nancy	304
Witt, Mary E.	557	Witt, Nancy	341
Witt, Mary E.	595	Witt, Nancy	356
Witt, Mary Etta	902	Witt, Nancy	367
Witt, Mary Jane	277	Witt, Nancy	519

Witt, Nancy	99	Witt, Phoebe Ann	442
Witt, Nancy A.	588	Witt, Phyllis C.	1107
Witt, Nancy A.	596	Witt, Piety	195
Witt, Nancy Candice	293	Witt, Pleasant	204
Witt, Nancy E.	449	Witt, Polly	130
Witt, Nancy Frances	1047	Witt, Polly	365
Witt, Nannie	716	Witt, Polly (Mary ?)	193
Witt, Nanny	490	Witt, Polly Ann	440
Witt, Nathan	147	Witt, Pool	298
Witt, Nathan Samuel	1207	Witt, Pool	66
Witt, Nathaniel	209	Witt, Prissa	348
Witt, Nell	630	Witt, Rachel	148
Witt, Nellie C.	346	Witt, Rachel	578
Witt, Nelly	106	Witt, Rachel	75
Witt, Nelson	161	Witt, Rachelle	1287
Witt, Newton	784	Witt, Randall Wayne	1226
Witt, Nicholas	1145	Witt, Rebecca	100
Witt, Nicholas Eric	1199	Witt, Rebecca	307
Witt, Noah	187	Witt, Rebecca	359
Witt, Noah H.	587	Witt, Rebecca	437
Witt, Nora	805	Witt, Rebecca Kay	1161
Witt, Norman Lee	1023	Witt, Rebecca Lynn	1316
Witt, Oakie	801	Witt, Regina	973
Witt, Obediah	158	Witt, Res ?	214
Witt, Ola Mae	987	Witt, Rhoda	108
Witt, Omer	922	Witt, Rhoda G.	234
Witt, Opal D.	931	Witt, Rhoda Susan	667
Witt, Ora M.	722	Witt, Richard	5
Witt, Orcia	800	Witt, Richard Daniel (Dan)	1313
Witt, Orvel Wayne	1033	Witt, Richard III	81
Witt, Orville Clifton	1065	Witt, Richard Jr.	21
Witt, Oscar	825	Witt, Robert	180
Witt, Oscar Grayson	720	Witt, Robert	24
Witt, Oscar Jr.	929	Witt, Robert	340
Witt, Otha	816	Witt, Robert	579
Witt, Otis	793	Witt, Robert	686
Witt, Owen O.	654	Witt, Robert Brooke	1084
Witt, Pamela Marie	1312	Witt, Robert Douglas	1205
Witt, Parker	632	Witt, Robert E.	717
Witt, Patsy Dale Patty	1241	Witt, Robert Hezikiah	732
Witt, Patsy Elizabeth	211	Witt, Robert L.	296
Witt, Patty	1264	Witt, Robert Oldridge	906
Witt, Paul Maward	1052	Witt, Robert R.	497
Witt, Pauline J.	1022	Witt, Robert Vernon	658
Witt, Pearlie	899	Witt, Robert W.	1095
Witt, Peter	67	Witt, Roberta	1059

Witt, Rodney	949	Witt, Sarah	475
Witt, Roger	1234	Witt, Sarah	651
Witt, Roger Clark	1201	Witt, Sarah	8
Witt, Roland	516	Witt, Sarah A.	399
Witt, Ronald	1143	Witt, Sarah Ann	295
Witt, Ronald Clifton	1211	Witt, Sarah Ann	517
Witt, Ronald Patrick	1314	Witt, Sarah Elizabeth	590
Witt, Ronald Ross	1202	Witt, Sarah Ella	479
Witt, Roy	917	Witt, Sarah Francis	343
Witt, Roy Jr.	1101	Witt, Sarah J.	429
Witt, Roy M.	542	Witt, Sarah J.	466
Witt, Roza B.	570	Witt, Sarah Jane	529
Witt, Ruby	786	Witt, Sarah L.	457
Witt, Ruby	813	Witt, Sarah Mandy	577
Witt, Ruby Mae	1046	Witt, Seth	299
Witt, Rushia	781	Witt, Sharon Rena	999
Witt, Ruth	812	Witt, Sherry Neal	1093
Witt, Ruth	983	Witt, Shirley Diane	965
Witt, Ruthy	79	Witt, Shirley Ilene	988
Witt, Ryan	1301	Witt, Sidney W.	508
Witt, Sadie	684	Witt, Silas	151
Witt, Sallie	270	Witt, Silas	196
Witt, Sallie	276	Witt, Silas	215
Witt, Sallie	488	Witt, Silvanus (Silas)	7
Witt, Sallie	505	Witt, Silvie	680
Witt, Sallie	97	Witt, Sonja	950
Witt, Sallie Mae	910	Witt, Sonya Kay	1183
Witt, Sally	171	Witt, Stanley Pete	835
Witt, Sally	176	Witt, Steven	1144
Witt, Sally	216	Witt, Steven Dexter	1193
Witt, Sally (Frances)	1021	Witt, Steven Paul	1157
Witt, Sally E.	827	Witt, Sue	803
Witt, Samuel	205	Witt, Susan	272
Witt, Samuel	405	Witt, Susan Bell	673
Witt, Samuel Alfred	1014	Witt, Susanna	280
Witt, Samuel H. Rev.	235	Witt, Susannah	109
Witt, Samuel Joseph	613	Witt, Tabitha	305
Witt, Samuel Joseph Jr.	814	Witt, Teresa	1254
Witt, Samuel W.	1040	Witt, Teresa L.	1120
Witt, Sandra	808	Witt, Thenia	83
Witt, Sarah	101	Witt, Thomas	503
Witt, Sarah	115	Witt, Thomas Jefferson	446
Witt, Sarah	136	Witt, Timothy Ray	1311
Witt, Sarah	14	Witt, Timothy Wayne	1185
Witt, Sarah	303	Witt, Tommy	574
Witt, Sarah	380	Witt, Tonya Renee	1182

Works Cited

Allen County, KY, Census Records, 1840-1910. National Archives Microfilm.

Allen County, KY, Census Records, 1920. Bureau of the Census Microfilm Laboratory.

Allen County, KY, Deed Books G, H, and M. Housed in the Clerk's Office, City-County Building, Scottsville, KY.

Allen County, KY, Marriage Records. Housed in the Clerk's Office, City-County Building, Scottsville, KY.

Allen County, KY, Tax Lists. National Archives Microfilm.

Baldridge, Blance Hamlett. *My Virginia Kin.*. Strawberry Point, Iowa: Press-Journal Pub. Co., 1958.

Barren County, KY, Census Records, 1850. National Archives Microfilm.

Barren County, KY, Census Records, 1860. Transcribed by H. Dana Harrison. Glasgow, KY: Gorin Genealogical Publishing, 1994.

Barren County, KY, Census Records, 1880. Soundex. Kentucky Department for Libraries and Archives. Frankfort, KY.

Barren County, KY, Marriage Records. Housed in Clerk's Office, Courthouse, Glasgow, KY.

Bates, Wayne Witt. "The Orphans of Walter Daux of Charles City County, Virginia." *The Huguenot Publication No. 27 (1975-1977)*. Published by The Huguenot Society Founders of Manakin, VA.

- - -. A Researcher in Centreville, VA. <wittbates@aol.com>.

Chamberlayne, Churchill Gibson, comp. *Births from the Bristol Parish Registry of Henrico, Prince George, and Dinwiddie Counties, VA, 1720-1798*. Baltimore: Genealogical Pub. Co., 1974.

Douglas Register, The. Ed. W. Mac Jones. Baltimore: Genealogical Pub. Co., 1966.

Gardner, Jeanetta Steenbergen, comp. *Allen County Kentucky Funeral Records*. Ozark, MO: Dogwood Printing, 1996.

Gendex: A Surname Database. <www.gendex.com>.

Gorin, Sandra K. *Barren County, Kentucky, Will Book 3.* Unpublished Report, 1991.

- - -. *Bible and Family Records, Barren County, KY.* Vol. 2. Unpublished Report, 1990.

- - -. *Deaths & Obituaries, Barren County, Kentucky, and Surrounding Areas. Vol. 2 M-Z.* Unpublished Report, 1990.

- - -. *Marriages of Barren County, KY, 1850-1860.* Unpublished Report, ND.

Graham, Marjorie Clark. *The Witt Family.* Unpublished Report, 1961.

Harbour-Witt Bulletin, ed. Bettye Cartwright, 6.2 (Fall 1983).

Hughes, Thomas P., Jr., and Jewel B. Standefer, comps. *Goochlard County, VA, Marriage Bonds and Minister's Returns, 1816-1854.* Memphis: Thomas P. Hughes, Jr., 1972.

Kentucky Vital Statistics. Frankfort, KY: Department for Human resources. Microfiche.

Laningham, Anne M. Wynn. *Early Settlers of Lee County, Virginia, and Adjacent Counties.* Vol. 1. Greensboro, NC: Media, 1977.

Leech, Brice T., and Kenneth Beard, eds. *Barren County, Kentucky, Cemetery Records.* Glasgow, KY: South Central Kentucky Historical and Genealogical Society, 1992.

Lombardo, Wanda. A Researcher in Richmond, KY. <llombardo@iclub.org>.

Norton, Mary Latham. Unpublished Manuscript.

Sweeny, Lenora. *Amherst County, VA, in the Revolution.* Berryville, VA: Virginia Book Co., 1951.

Sweeny, William Montgomery. *Marriage Bonds and other Marriage Records of Amherst County, VA, 1763-1800.* Baltimore: Genealogical Pub. Co., 1973.

Vogt, John, and T. William Kethley, Jr. *Nelson County Marriages 1808-1830.* Athens, GA: Iberian Press, 1985.

Watkins, Sherry. A Researcher in Louisville, KY. <Parabannon@aol.com>.

Weisiger, Benjamin B., III. *Charles City County, VA, Court Orders, 1687-1695.* NP, 1980.

- - -. *Charles City County, VA, Wills and Deeds, 1725-1731.* NP, 1984.

- - -. *Colonial Wills of Henrico County, VA, Part One 1654-1737.* NP, 1976.

- - -. *Goochland County Wills and Deeds, 1728-36.* NP, 1983.

- - -. *Goochland County Wills and Deeds, 1736-42.* NP, 1984.

- - -. *Henrico County, VA, Deeds, 1706-1737.* Richmond, VA: NP, 1985.

Whitt, Jane C. "John Witt/Whitt of Charles City County, Virginia, and Four of his Sons." *The Huguenot Publication No. 32 (1985-1987).* Published by the Huguenot Society Founders of Manakin, VA.

Williams, Kathleen, comp. *Marriages of Goodchland County, VA, 1733-1815.* Baltimore: Genealogical Pub. Co., 1979.

Williams, Louis J., and William Tyler Ross. *The Harbours in America.* Lubbock, TX: Harbour-Harbor-Harber Family Association, 1982.

Witt, Larry. A Researcher in Somerset, KY. <photo@som-uky.campus.mci.net>.

Made in the USA